# WALKING
## IN THE
# FOOTSTEPS
## OF THE RABBI
## FROM TARSUS

### JEFFREY L. SEIF

# In the Footsteps of the Rabbi from Tarsus

ISBN 978-1-930749-46-7

# Dedication

To my lovely wife, Patty.

We met in our youth, and have gone down
life's highway together all these years.

For making the journey with me,
for carving out a path with me,
and for being a guiding light and compass—
*My helpmate and very best friend,*
*this book is dedicated to you.*

# Table of Contents

## Introducing the Rabbi from Tarsus
Introducing Paul ...................................................1
Introducing This New Book on Paul........................7
The Book's Method........................................17
Special Thanks................................................18


## I. Paul's Perplexing World
Introduction ........................................................21
Bizarre Roman Mythologies,
    Philosophies, and Religions.........................24
The Roman Pantheon.........................................25
Prophetic Unction in Roman Culture....................27
Healing Cults in Roman Culture
    *Asclepius* ..............................................31
Ecstatic Cults in Roman Culture
    *Dionysus*.............................................32
    *Atargatis* ............................................33
Sexual Impropriety in Roman Culture...................34


## II. The *Acts* of the Apostle Paul
Introduction .....................................................45
Emergence of the Messianic Rabbi from Tarsus ..46
Overview of Luke's Pauline Texts ............................48
Paul's Conversion and Preparation............................53
    Acts 9-12

# Table of Contents

Paul's First Journey, 46-48AD ............... 61
Acts 13-14
Trip to Jerusalem, ca. 37-38AD ............... 73
Acts 15:4-15:29
Paul's Second Journey, 49-52AD ............... 78
Acts 15:36-18:22
Paul's Third Journey, 53-57AD ............... 94
Acts 18:23-21:15
Trip to Jerusalem, ca. 48-49AD ............... 108
Acts 21:16-26:32
Paul's Fourth Journey, 59-62AD ............... 131
Acts 27:1-28:31


## III. The *Facts* of the Apostle Paul
Introduction ............... 143
### 1. Paul's Letter to the Church at Galatia
Introductory Overview ............... 145
Important Interpretations ............... 149
Contemporary Applications ............... 153
Personal Applications ............... 155
### 2. Paul's 1st Letter to the Church at Thessalonica
Introductory Overview ............... 157
Important Interpretations ............... 158
Contemporary Applications ............... 160
Personal Applications ............... 163
### 3. Paul's 2nd Letter to the Church at Thessalonica
Introductory Overview ............... 166
Important Interpretations ............... 168
Contemporary Applications ............... 170
Personal Applications ............... 172

# Table of Contents

4. **Paul's 1st Letter to the Church at Corinth**
   Introductory Overview .......................................... 174
   Important Interpretations ..................................... 175
   Contemporary Applications .................................. 183
   Personal Applications........................................... 186
5. **Paul's 2nd Letter to the Church at Corinth**
   Introductory Overview .......................................... 189
   Important Interpretations ..................................... 191
   Contemporary Applications .................................. 194
   Personal Applications........................................... 198
6. **Paul's Letter to the Christians in Rome**
   Introductory Overview .......................................... 200
   Important Interpretations ..................................... 204
   Contemporary Applications .................................. 207
   Personal Applications........................................... 210
7. **Paul's Letter to Philemon**
   Introductory Overview .......................................... 212
   Important Interpretations ..................................... 212
   Contemporary Applications .................................. 214
   Personal Applications........................................... 216
8. **Paul's Letter to the Church at Colosse**
   Introductory Overview .......................................... 218
   Important Interpretations ..................................... 218
   Contemporary Applications .................................. 220
   Personal Applications........................................... 221
9. **Paul's Letter to the Church at Ephesus**
   Introductory Overview .......................................... 223
   Important Interpretations ..................................... 224
   Contemporary Applications .................................. 227
   Personal Applications........................................... 230

# Table of Contents

10. **Paul's Letter to the Church at Philippi**
    Introductory Overview..............................232
    Important Interpretations.........................234
    Contemporary Applications........................237
    Personal Applications ............................240
11. **Paul's 1st Letter to Timothy**
    Introductory Overview..............................242
    Important Interpretations.........................242
    Contemporary Applications........................248
    Personal Applications ............................253
12. **Paul's Letter to Titus**
    Introductory Overview..............................255
    Important Interpretations.........................255
    Contemporary Applications........................256
    Personal Applications ............................260
13. **Paul's 2nd Letter to Timothy**
    Introductory Overview..............................262
    Important Interpretations.........................262
    Contemporary Applications........................263
    Personal Applications ............................263


**Conclusion**
    Final Reflections on
        Pauline Faith and Practice..........................267

# Introducing the Rabbi from Tarsus

## Introducing Paul

Who was Paul? What was he like? Where was he from? Where did he go and why? How did he get there? How did someone like him—a man who was *not* part of the original apostolic community—link up with the first Apostles and eventually become their movement's principal advocate? Why was he considered an "outsider" by many ancient Believers, and not taken particularly seriously? Why should we modern Believers take him seriously today? This book will consider these and other related questions as we enter into Paul's world, become reacquainted with him, and walk in the footsteps of this famous Jewish Rabbi from Tarsus.

Rabbi Paul—originally known as Rabbi Saul, known later as the Apostle Paul—was "converted" around 34 or 35AD—

possibly earlier. In the wake of his providential encounter with the One whom he rightly came to construe as Israel's Messiah, Paul went to Damascus and then to Arabia, from 35-37AD. This route bypassed Judea—with its Messianic Jewish elders and teachers—with the result that he had no official link to the apostolic tradition.

Three years after his initial experience with Yeshua (Jesus), the Messianic rabbi went to Jerusalem for his first "official" visit, during which time he met with some of the fledgling Messianic movement's "official" leaders. After a very brief sojourn there, the Rabbi from Tarsus went to, and appears to have hibernated in, Tarsus and Cilicia from 37-45AD, until he made his way to Jerusalem.

While this book will consider Paul's travels in detail, let me first give you a brief overview to acquaint you with his chronology. On his first apostolic and "missionary" journey, Paul traveled during the period from 46-48AD after he was dispatched from Antioch, Syria. Though he enjoyed measured progress, all was not well; for after returning from his first apostolic adventure, Paul was forced back to Jerusalem in 48-49 to answer questions that had arisen in response to his controversial ministry. With that uncomfortable business attended to, a vindicated Paul embarked on his second apostolic journey, which extended from around 49-52. His third and longest missionary trip lasted from 53-57, after which he again returned to his beloved Jerusalem where things got out of hand once more, and a riot ensued. In the wake of the civic unrest, Paul was arrested and incarcerated in

# Introduction

Caesarea from 57-59. His appeal to Rome to redress his grievances resulted in his being sent there by ship on an arduous journey that extended from 59-60. Imprisoned in Rome from 60-62, he awaited trial and was apparently released on the assumption of a positive outcome. Apparently, Paul then ministered in the east from 62-64 until he was arrested, imprisoned, and finally beheaded by Nero in 64 or 65. So there they are, his travels in a nutshell.

Because he moved about swiftly, and in order to respond to a variety of pressing circumstances that confronted him and the church communities he'd established, Paul wrote a variety of instructional letters, wherein he offered advice on a variety of subjects. Thirteen of these letters were collected and preserved in what became known as the New Testament, under what scholars call the "Pauline Corpus"—the body of literature that bears Paul's influence. As we consider the rabbi's travels, we'll also unpack his various writings in some detail.

That Rabbi Paul became very influential as a churchman is both striking and unexpected. He was initially hell-bent on Christianity's demise; that he "switched gears" and actually joined the Jesus movement is striking. That he became its most forceful advocate is unexpected because, of all the Apostles, he arguably knew the least about Jesus' life and teachings, having had no firsthand knowledge. That he didn't go immediately to Judea and get the benefit of that knowledge is, itself, quite interesting.

# In the Footsteps of the Rabbi from Tarsus

Many felt he was unqualified. This book will address that issue, as well as how he overcame their objections. Despite his critics, Paul occupies center stage in the New Testament, where he serves as its principal theologian. I find that fascinating and worthy of investigation.

Though Paul rose to be the Church's principal expert on Christian faith and practice, his writings rarely note any of Jesus' events, nor do they quote His sayings or parables. Why not? Likely it was because Paul knew not! Remember, he wasn't an original apostle and had no firsthand knowledge.

So why Paul? What did he know?

His incorporating in his letters almost one hundred quotations from the Old Testament attests to the Jewish Bible's inestimable value in his mind and its residence in his heart. Though in one certain sense he didn't know Jesus in life—as the other Apostles did—Paul did encounter Him, was filled with His Spirit, and was helped by some of the early brethren, like Barnabas. Led by the Spirit through a rather unique revelation, Paul came to know that Jesus' death, burial, and resurrection inaugurated a new era in the human experience—the era of the Messianic Kingdom. Even with his limitations, the Spirit-filled Paul advocated for the Jewish "Kingdom" in deed and in word. Although it not might seem logical that he would rise as he did, his emergence was obviously providential.

# Introduction

Thirteen of Paul's letters, spanning a career of some fifteen years, have come down to us. These are the best sources available for understanding Paul's actual message, his methods, and his movements. I believe there is great value in studying these, and by refracting them through a decidedly Jewish prism—which happens to be a Zola Levitt Ministries trademark.

Many well-intended Christians miss Paul's key points when they force him to sound like an ex-Jew and/or a "converted Jew." Interpreters who try to explain this Rabbi from Tarsus while stripping him of his worldview and culture do a disservice to Paul, to his writings, to themselves, and to their audience.

Paul was not a "converted Jew" or some sort of "ex-Jew," as is typically proffered today. The Rabbi from Tarsus didn't get down on his knees and ask God to forgive him for being Jewish. He asked God to forgive him for his *sins*: for rejecting Jesus and discriminating against His followers. Being Jewish was no sin! After all, Jesus was Jewish too. Paul was a converted *sinner*. He lived, functioned, and thought like a Jew until his dying day.

Those who journey with me *In the Footsteps of the Rabbi from Tarsus* will come to appreciate what the Jewish Paul looked and sounded like before he became the modern, Catholic "St. Paul," the Baptist "Brother Paul," the Lutheran Paul, etc. I am interested in stripping away the accretions imposed upon Paul by well-intended,

# In the Footsteps of the Rabbi from Tarsus

modern interpreters and discovering him in his own Jewish context, wherein we'll hear him advocating for—and not against—decidedly Jewish experiences and practices.

These somewhat academic considerations aside, let me speak pastorally and say that individuals in the modern "high tech" world and Church have a crying need—whether they consciously know it or not—to earnestly return to what I tentatively call primitive "Christian" faith and practice. I believe readers will derive benefit from this book's contents, given its emphasis on getting at the heart and substance of authentic Pauline "Christianity," and by getting at it from a decidedly Jewish vantage point.

Paul's writings are the premiere apostolic source of biblical medicine for soul-sickened humanity's assorted hurts. As such, they hold out personal promise to those perplexed by stressful circumstances and beset by attendant anxieties. Paul brings hope that one can get the better of one's circumstances and attitudes. Furthermore, and harking back to my previous point, looking at Paul's helpful writings with a Jewish set of eyes opens up inter-pretive options that enable readers to better understand the man, his context, his message's content, and what God says through it.

I am anxious to introduce you to the real Paul, a Messianic Jewish rabbi from the ancient, first-century Hellenistic-Jewish world.

# Introduction

Academic theology, the sort that I engage in here, doesn't typically enjoy great favor within the "pop" element in the Church where fads historically take precedence over standard, biblical exposition. However, I believe that sin-surrounded Christian people may be soul-sickened to the point where they are willing to labor a bit to rediscover an authentic, biblical New Testament worldview and walk.

I propose to extract from neglected, sacred, biblical literature and include in but one small book, the essence and substance of the Messianic life as taught by the ancient rabbi-turned-reverend from Tarsus—the "Apostle" Paul.

In a world where too many ministers "dumb down" the Gospel's requirements (in hopes of increasing church attendance), prophetically clarifying the essence and substance of authentic faith and practice as defined by Paul, at both individual and congregational levels, seems timely for a variety of reasons, which I will briefly delineate now.

## Introducing This New Book on Paul

Readers of this book can expect to be personally confronted and challenged through a forthright engagement with Paul's practical theology. I will do this without apology, realizing that I may well offend someone. *C'est la vie!*

Many in our churches are either ignorant of the essential requirements of authentic biblical faith and practice, or are aware but simply not interested in practicing the faith they claim and ostensibly embrace. Perhaps more importantly, many in our socially "churched," postmodern culture do not really know the essence of the faith as distilled by the Apostle Paul. Or, some may have known a small part of it at one point, but over time, authentic faith and practice tragically drifted from thought and application, into distant memories. All these cause me to see value in offering a coherent retelling of the original Pauline faith and practice. Though two thousand years old, it is "Good News" for modern women and men.

Demographic studies show that fornication, adultery, idolatry, lying, stealing, and covetousness abound in our churches—among professing Christians—and at levels similar to those in the general, secular culture. This is perplexing and cause for reflection. Does this alone not demonstrate that many professing Christians need a reminder of the moral requirements of the Christian faith? Whatever the spiritual condition of the culture generally, or of you the reader particularly, I wrote this book convinced that we each can benefit by reviewing Paul's world and words, his words being the basic Christian principles.

Mindful of these needs, interests, and questions, we will examine every book written by the Apostle Paul, following the chronological order in which they are understood to have been written (taking our lead from

# Introduction

Acts) and not the canonical order of their appearance in our New Testament (which is longest to shortest).

Reconstructing Paul's life and career in narrative form will assist us in exposing and considering his decidedly Jewish teachings. Paul's thirteen documents, which each contain important instructions for both congregational and individual Christian commitments, will be outlined briefly in narrative form, with special attention given to issues and principles he addressed.

Sound meaningful? I hope so, because I think it is important—very important.

Because the Bible is the authoritative source for Judeo-Christian religious instruction, one may wonder why a book of this nature is even necessary. Believers can benefit by simply reading the Scripture—and I highly endorse that practice. Nevertheless, I believe there is room for a formal theological treatment of those passages that relate to Christians' individual faithfulness and congregations' commitments—especially when designed to help individuals recover the long-lost Jewish roots of their Christian faith.

The Old Testament contains 39 books, which are broken into 929 chapters, 23,214 verses and 593,493 words. The New Testament has a total of 27 books, 260 chapters, 7,959 verses and 181,253 words. Combined, the Bible contains 66 books, 1,189 chapters, 31,173 verses, and a total of 774,746 words. Again, while there is merit in simply giving someone a Bible and saying "read it and grow," there is also value in providing a condensed, easy-to-understand assessment of the Bible's message and meaning. That is the purpose of this particular book. I hope that its Jewish perspective generates more interest and meaning for my readers.

Paul—the ancient rabbi-turned-reverend—was the official "apostolic" interpreter of the Old Testament in the New Testament. He was also the New Testament's primary author and theologian, vested with responsibility to interpret the implications of the life of the Messiah for all who would hear him—Jews and non-Jews alike.

What did the rabbi say?

Paul said that individual human beings are "called" to personal conversion and salvation (Romans 8:28-30) and to sanctification (1 Thessalonians 4:3 and 5:23-24). He advocated separation from unbelievers (2 Corinthians 6:14-18) and even anticipated suffering (Acts 14:22, Philippians 1:29 and 3:10, and 1 Thessalonians 3:3). In Philippians 2:1-18 and Ephesians 2:10, he instructed Believers to place a premium on service.

According to Paul, in addition to being called to personal salvation and sanctification, Believers in Christ are also called to a life of corporate participation in service. In fact, the Messiah actually assesses the extent to which

# Introduction

individuals link up and participate in His Kingdom's purposes, meting out rewards to individuals accordingly.

Paul said that Believers are endowed with natural and even supernaturally-given abilities, and the degree to which Christians employ their newly constituted energies and talents is the object of Christ's assessment at day's end, as noted in 1 Corinthians 12:4, 12:11, and 2 Timothy 1:6. Biblical perspectives lead us to these and other related understandings. We do well to acquaint ourselves with the biblical instruction.

Jesus Himself went on record in Matthew's Gospel, closing His "Last Supper" teaching with three parables, each extremely important. Matthew 25:1-13 emphasizes the preparedness of maidens, or the lack thereof (vv. 8-10). Similarly, in Matthew 25:14-30 Jesus told of various types of stewards, one of whom was negligent in his duties, resulting in his being "cast into the outer darkness" (v. 30). The theme of negligence continues in vv. 31-46 with the story of the "sheep and the goats" in which the shepherd sorted out the sincere from the insincere on the basis of their participation in helping to alleviate the suffering of others (vv. 34-46).

For these and other reasons, it seems that the Messiah saves people for a purpose, and that individuals are evaluated on the extent to which they dedicate themselves to that purpose.

# In the Footsteps of the Rabbi from Tarsus

Being "salt" and "light" in this world (Matthew 5:13-17)—to actually affect and guide perplexed people—is apparently of primary importance to Jesus, despite its diminished popularity in our constellation of conflicted, self-centered concerns.

Simply "going to church" is not a sufficient basis to assess one's Christian life and contribution to Christ's Kingdom. Unadulterated kindness toward others, however, apparently does factor significantly in Christ's economy. How authorities employ power enjoys special consideration in Hebrews 13:17; how Believers treat others generally, merits special concern in Hebrews 13:1-3, Matthew 10:41-42, and elsewhere.

Much as interpersonal affairs seem to matter, intrapersonal ones do too. Paul instructs followers of Christ to be good stewards of their time (Ephesians 5:16, Colossians 4:5) and of their money. Jesus' saying "where your treasure is, there will your heart be also" (Matthew 6:21) is especially significant, given that the way we make and spend money provides a window into our real values—and not just the values we might pay lip service to on a Sunday when, lacking a better offer, we happen to show up in church. Using money for noble purposes was important to Paul (1 Corinthians 16:2, 2 Corinthians 9:6-7, and 1 Timothy 6:17-19).

Time management, to a certain degree, should involve Scripture study: We're exhorted to study biblical literature and doctrine because doing so saves us from deceit

# Introduction

(1 Timothy 4:13-16), much as Ephesians 4:14 says it helps settle us internally. Paul said in 2 Timothy 3:13-17 and in Ephesians 6:10-18 that good doctrine equips us to attend to the business described in the paragraphs above.

Biblical exhortations toward brotherly love, virtue, and faith-based commitments seem to have fallen on deaf ears in our perplexed, religion-saturated culture, evidenced by the fact that professing Christians disappoint, betray, and abandon each other with a brazen impunity that is increasing at alarming rates. It comes as no surprise, then, that genuine individual and local church commitment is diminishing in the North American Christian experience.

We need to hear from the Rabbi from Tarsus!

The lack of social cohesion in many sectors of the Christian community must be seen as part of a broader, social problem. Much as modern people generally seem to forever renegotiate their employment, their residences, and tragically, even their families, restless Christians—who also seem unable to find the deep-seated satisfaction they long for—are predisposed to move from job to job, from relational partner to partner, and from church to church. Many are perplexed and invest a considerable amount of energy running nowhere fast—like mice on an endless treadmill. Indeed, many restless Christians seem more like treadmill mice than like calmed sheep, dedicated to discerning their Shepherd's voice, attending to His commands, and following His particular directions—along with other like-minded individuals.

# In the Footsteps of the Rabbi from Tarsus

An indication of this is how people used to speak of their congregation as their "church home"—now an anachronistic expression. Perhaps we ought to speak instead of our "church apartment." Odd though it sounds, this may be more correct. Though there are some exceptions, apartments tend to be rented by individuals needing a temporary place, who don't want the commitments and responsibilities of home ownership. Leases tend to be as short-term as possible. People want "in" with as little "down" as possible. Apartment dwellings most often are briefly inhabited by people until they can find something that will better serve their evolving needs and restless interests.

"Church apartment" may be more accurate and descriptive than "church home," but this *still* may be granting too much stability to socially inept Western Christians. Sad to say, people might speak even more accurately if they referred to their "church hotel." And why is that? The present "stay" in a church for many Americans is extremely short. Like hotel lodgers, they feel entitled to make a mess, expecting someone else to come and clean it up after they've moved on in their restless quest for another place to temporarily dwell—to a more "perfect" church. Does the problem lie with the church body, or is it in the mind of the restless seeker?

I think there is something terribly wrong with our dysfunctional, "entitlement thinking." Christian "mice" stuck on the destructive treadmill would better serve themselves, their communities, and their Messiah if they

# Introduction

were to find a way off the treadmill through a fresh reconsideration of Paul's essential teachings on what it means to walk with the Messiah. The "church to church" movement—or "church hopping" as it is cutely referred to—is the Christian version of the diseased social deterioration that prevails in our post-modern culture. Most Christians realize this; but because they are out of control, they are not sure how to stop the process of decay in themselves or in others.

There is, of course, no discoverable "perfect" social refuge—family or church—wherein one can happily live out one's life, undisturbed by the thorny problems of precarious human conflicts and experiences. If people have tried relationships with twelve different women/men or twelve different churches and not found what they desire, should they think that they will "luck out" with the thirteenth relationship or the thirteenth church? I don't think so. I fear that the primary problem is in the thought-process of the seeker, and not in the environment.

What do you think? Is the perennial dissatisfaction and the quest for perfection external or internal?

If the problem is *external*, then the answer may indeed be "out there," and folk ought to keep abandoning the old and seeking the new. If, however, it is *internal* and located somewhere in the way we think, then it will not be found "out there" in interpersonal relationships because the problem is *intra*personal, that is, it is within the person seeking the relief. If the problem is in our own thought processes, the external quest for perfection is futile because we take our wrong thinking with us everywhere we search, and therefore always come up disappointed. People need a biblical worldview to be saved from this dysfunctional process.

The expression "going to church," which is typically used for attending Sunday morning services, betrays a serious deficiency in our thinking. In Scripture, a church is not a *place*—with stained glass windows, pipe organs, collection boxes, and pews—but a *community*: social relationships between individuals who are giving up on selfish individuality's false hopes and promises; who at ever-increasing levels invest personal energy and resources in community-oriented, Christian faith and practice.

There is no perfect church house somewhere out there, much as there is no perfect spouse out there just waiting to be discovered and save the discoverer. Happily, however, there really is a perfect answer to life's relentless problems. The answer is not abandoning old people and exchanging them for new; the real answer is exchanging old ideas for new, *biblical* ideas.

People do have problems in their thought processes—the lack of a biblical process being foremost among them. It is imperative that we replace our natural thought process toward "stinking" with biblical approaches toward cogent "thinking."

# Introduction

We do well to soak in biblical perspectives, let the Holy Spirit gently instruct us, and allow the Lord to raise us up as "new creations" to be the women and men He has called us to be—and that means being different from others in our prevailing, dysfunctional, post-modern culture. This, of course, is a work that only the Lord can do. Jesus is the answer. But I can assist you to better understand Him and the life He advocated, by providing a fresh engagement with His principal interpreter—Paul.

## The Book's Method
I believe that a perplexed world can use another book on basic Christianity, so this book will serve as a "primer," as an introduction to "basic Christianity," and as a guide for the perplexed.

The brief chapter that follows, Chapter I ("Paul's Perplexing World"), gives readers a window into Paul's bizarre and fractured world—an ancient setting that was, interestingly, akin to our own. This is done through an abridged treatment of ancient Roman deities, mythologies, philosophies, and religions.

Chapter II ("The *Acts* of the Apostle Paul") relates a descriptive treatment of Paul's travels, followed by Chapter III ("The *Facts* of the Apostle Paul"), a prescriptive treatment of biblical Texts—a brief analysis of Paul's remedial and inspired words.

# In the Footsteps of the Rabbi from Tarsus

A Bible teacher above all else, I aim to expose readers to biblical narrative and instruction, believing that the exposure itself helps individuals set their moral compasses and make adjustments if necessary.

## Special Thanks

I would like to pay special thanks to Marcelo Guimaraes and Mattheus Guimaraes, who invited me to teach in Belo Horizonte, Brazil, at the Messianic Jewish Bible Institute at Associacao Ministerio Ensinando de Siao, during which time I was able to develop the first draft of this book. I used that draft to teach a summer school course entitled "Introduction to Pauline Literature" at Christ for the Nations Institute in Dallas, Texas, and was able to refine the book then, and again when I used the workbook to lead a mini-series at Grace Community Church in Houston, Texas, at the invitation of my friend and mentor Pastor Steve Riggle. I am greatly indebted to Bryan Binder's assistance with the editorial process. I finally was able to get the book in its finished form through my work with Zola Levitt Ministries, where it is offered in conjunction with a television series, *In the Footsteps of the Rabbi from Tarsus*, in which I chronicle some of Paul's travels and principal teachings. I especially thank ZLM's editor Margot Dokken and Greg Hartwig for their valuable editorial assistance. Without their help, I simply would not be able to communicate as clearly as I would like.

# Introduction

That my wife Patty, along with our fine sons Jacob and Zachary, gave me leave to attend to this is, as always, a credit to their virtues, and cause for particular special mention herein as well.

Given that without her support this book would not have been written, nor my life productive to the extent that it is, I am pleased to dedicate this book to my wife Patty— a woman who has never written a book, nor graduated from a seminary, but who knows more about the Lord and the Christian life than I do.

Jeffrey L. Seif                                    Zurich, Switzerland

# I

## Paul's Perplexing World

### Introduction

When "Rabbi" Paul opted to (1) step *up* and be a so-called "Christian" apostle, to (2) step *out* beyond Judea to advance the Messianic Kingdom, and then to (3) step *into* the Greco-Roman world to attend to apostolic business, what kind of moral and philosophical world did he leave behind, and what sort of world did he enter? These questions are necessary first-steps toward coming to terms with Paul's teaching.

# In the Footsteps of the Rabbi from Tarsus

Basically, Paul left a biblically informed *Jewish world* when he stepped out to bring biblical vision and virtue to a *non-Jewish, pagan world.* Unlike many of his apostolic contemporaries, Paul worked with relative comfort in the non-Jewish world, environments that had non-biblical and even anti-biblical standards—some of which were reprehensible.

To assist with religious education, the Jews in Paul's day had the "Torah"—the Hebrew Scriptures. Non-Jews, in the Jews' estimation, had nothing worthwhile—at least nothing of significant ethical and spiritual substance. Without an authoritative, value-centered philosophical base, the moral and spiritual landscape of the ancient Greeks and Romans was, as we shall see, checkered with assorted grotesque and immoral personal practices, coupled with a host of ghastly and absurd religious rituals. Lacking the value-rich religious underpinnings of the Hebrews with their revealed Scriptures, Roman citizens inhabited a bizarre and morally rudderless world, one that many dedicated "Torah observant" Jews, for various good reasons, condemned outright and protected themselves from, at all costs.

Mindful of Jesus' prayer (John 17:15-16) for his followers to be "in the world but not of it," Paul was somehow "in" the Roman world but not really part "of" it. Like many of his Jewish contemporaries, he opposed the myriad rank, moral perversions all around him; but he was still more comfortable than they were with Roman culture and thus cultivated relationships with non-Jews owing to

# Paul's Perplexing World

his more accepting disposition. Both a faithful Jew and a loyal and proud Roman citizen, Paul seemed more bent on gleaning a harvest among non-Jews, in lands far removed from Judea, than he was interested in simply decrying the pervasive bizarre religious and social practices that were common among non-Israelites in the broader pagan culture.

Paul had the Hebrew Scriptures as his guiding light. Biblically and spiritually enlightened, especially in the wake of his radical conversion and transformation, Paul eventually shared his personal experiences and theological findings with others—non-Jewish "others" particularly. Being accepting of non-Jews, and believing, perhaps, that it is better to light candles than to curse the darkness, *Paul distilled and married the essence of biblical Judaism with the substance of Israel's Messianic hope, and then found ways to creatively impregnate the broader non-Jewish culture with the fruits of the philosophical union.* Paul believed that God would use him to help Israel fulfill its destiny of becoming a "light unto the nations"—as the prophets had long envisioned—much as he could fulfill his personal destiny by participating in the bold apostolic enterprise of advancing God's Kingdom on this Earth.

To better understand Paul's project—the primary object of this book—we need to understand Paul's strange world, the stage upon which his story played out.

We live nearly two thousand years removed from Paul, chronologically. We are philosophically distant, as well—

# In the Footsteps of the Rabbi from Tarsus

because Paul's was a *non*-Christian world, whereas ours is a culture with nearly two thousand years of Christian influence. A great cultural divide separates us from Paul and the world of the New Testament. We will labor to bridge that gap.

The following introductory subsection on ancient religious practices and professions common in Paul's day is hardly exhaustive.[1] Though it is limited, I hope that the brief consideration will prove interesting and useful. It is sure to prove interesting because the bizarre can be counted on to be interesting. Its usefulness will be judged by whether it helps you better understand Paul's writings. Leaving that assessment until later, let us enter into a time machine and journey back to Paul's strange world, hoping to develop a better understanding of the Apostle and the message he delivered to its inhabitants—and to us.

## Bizarre Roman Mythologies, Philosophies, and Religions

Both Paul and the pagans of his day were interested in what was, to use a play on words, "right"/"rite." "*Right*," of course, speaks of moral correctness, and concerned Paul greatly. "*Rite*" speaks of ceremony and liturgy: rites were of primary importance to ancient Greeks and Romans, who were devoutly religious, but without the moral underpinnings of "rightness," so important to Paul

---

[1] See Everett Ferguson, *Backgrounds Of Early Christianity* (Eerdmans) for a more in-depth study. A portion of this chapter was also produced in my 2007 volume, *Guns & Moses*.

# Paul's Perplexing World

and his Jewish counterparts. Pharisees in Paul's day were concerned with what was "right"; Sadducees—inhabiting and managing the priestly Temple guilds—seemed more interested in ceremonial "rites," though they valued moral rightness also. Some Christian traditions emphasize "rites" (e.g., stylized liturgies) and moral "rightness"; some place more emphasis on moral rightness and less on rites. Romans, by way of contradistinction, were not morally inclined, though they were apparently quite fond of superstitious, ceremonial rites.

Why the rites? Ancient Roman cosmogony (theory of the world's creation) depicted humans as trapped in an unfriendly and uncharted universe, a strange supernatural world inhabited by myriads of potentially hazardous, unseen, demonic forces. As a defense against the prevailing uncertainty and darkness, Romans employed religious rituals to secure the favor and protection of their various gods. By appeasing their deities with "rites," they hoped to secure both their places in this world and their passage to the next one. Superstition was ubiquitous in antiquity, and the Romans attempted to assuage their religious anxieties by placating their various and sometimes ill-tempered divinities—some of whom were perceived as half-baked humans. Here is a brief description of the principal Roman mythological, human-like gods.

## The Roman Pantheon
Known as Zeus to the Greeks, and as Jupiter to the Romans, he was the heavenly father of the gods, president of the association of Olympian divines, and the patriarch

of the famous ancient Greek religious pantheon. Because—
like man—no god should be alone, he had a good godly
wife. Known as Hera to the Greeks, and as Juno to the
Romans, she was the wife of the patriarchal god and
came to be appropriately associated with marriage and
women. Unfortunately, as is the case with some mere
mortals, the divine Zeus had a problem with his wandering
libido—with adultery. Sexual encounters with mortal
women invoked the ire of Hera—but more on that later.

Other royal family members included Zeus' brother,
Poseidon, or Neptune as he was known to the Romans.
He was the god of the seas. Athena (Minerva to the
Romans) was Zeus' daughter. She was the virgin goddess
of wisdom and the arts, and was personally the protector
of Athens. Military motifs are associated with her, and
she was said to have sprung from Zeus' head at birth,
both fully grown and fully armed.

Apollo was distinguished among many as the "all Greek"
god/lad, the idealized Greek male, known for manly
beauty, music, archery, prophecy, medicine, flocks and
herds, law, civilization, and other staples of refined
culture. Apollo embodied the characteristics prized by
the Greeks. Apollo's twin sister, Artemis (Diana) was the
chaste goddess of the countryside, involved as a goddess
in childbirth. *She* may have been chaste, others in the
family were not: unbridled licentiousness and jealousy
seemed more the order of the day—even among the
Olympian divines. In fact, it was the Greek acceptance
and celebration of immodesty and sexual impropriety that

prompted Torah-observant Jews to disdain and condemn Hellenistic culture outright.

Both the Greeks and the Romans placed a premium on militancy and worshipped the god of war: Ares (Mars). Because courageous soldiers needed pleasure, they worshipped the god of wine: Dionysus (Bacchus). Hephaestus (Vulcan) was the god of fire and crafts, a manufacturing deity. Lastly, Hermes (Mercury) was the messenger of the gods, in addition to which he guarded roadways and even conducted souls to Hades (Pluto)—brother of Zeus (Jupiter) and god of the frightening abyss which was the Greek underworld.

## Prophetic Unction in Roman Culture

Individuals pleased their militant, lusty, and emotionally unstable gods and secured their place in the afterlife by varied means, such as a proper burial—considered very important lest the deceased Roman wander perpetually in a phantasmal, ghost-like state of unrest, never being afforded the peace granted to the dead who had been properly interred. The *Iliad* opened with souls being thrust into Hades, which was depicted as a dreary place where, according to Homer, life continued—but in a manner not worth living. One might avoid this dread non-existence by adhering to Roman religious tradition, which could purchase safe passage to the next world, much as it could enhance the passage through this one.

Believing that mortals could placate their various gods— and secure benefits for themselves as a result—ancient

# In the Footsteps of the Rabbi from Tarsus

Romans frequented temples and brought gifts and religious offerings. Greek and Roman temples even had treasury rooms to hold the various gifts that the faithful offered in the hopes of securing the gods' fancy on Olympus and their consequential favors on Earth beneath. It was *quid pro quo:* offer gifts, get something in return—a sign or an omen from the gods.

Ancient Greeks and Romans placed a premium on interpreting omens, and anxiously sought heavenly sanctions to address earthly questions and anxieties. As superstitious as the ancients apparently were, accessing heaven's powers in some form was important to them, and frequenting religious sanctuaries to consult oracles for prophetic messages was a popular activity—so popular that cities even sent official delegations to sacred shrines to inquire on matters of economics, war, and politics, as well as official religious matters. Religious sites were thus perceived as prophecy centers, and were widely employed to help citizens connect to their higher power. This was central in Roman pre-Christian belief systems.

Though there were various "daughter" sanctuaries, pride of place was given to the "mother house" at Delphi—considered to be Zeus' spot for the actual "center of the earth." This was the site where Apollo, the quintessential Greek warrior, had killed "Python"—a spectacular she-serpent, deemed an earth goddess in early Minoan (Bronze Age Crete) religion. For this reason, the heroic Apollo factored significantly at Delphi, where he was perceived as Zeus' representative. Though Apollo became the god of prophecy and a spokesman for Zeus at Delphi, it was a priestess who presided over Delphi's main religious attraction: prophetic oracle-giving. And she was a celibate priestess, as forgoing sexual activity was deemed a prerequisite to uttering prophetic words.

In Acts 16:16, Luke noted that "a certain slave girl possessed with a spirit of divination" annoyed Paul and Silas. Luke's Greek text specified that the "possessed" girl who badgered Paul was "possessed of a Pythian spirit." But by the 1600s, "Pythian" was an unfamiliar term, so the Bible's translators chose "spirit of divination" to point out that the ancient slave girl was known for being "possessed," and given to "prophetic oracles," or "divination." Describing the slave girl's divinations as "Pythian" is significant, however, because the celibate prophetess who presided at Delphi was known as a "Pythia." It is thus apparent that the slave girl in Luke's narrative was at least marginally related to the Delphi cult—many lesser known sites and prophetesses were located throughout much of the empire, taking their lead from the movement headquartered at Delphi. The slave girl was possibly from one of these "daughter" sites.

How did someone get a prophecy? What happened at Delphi—and at other oracle sites? At the temple, inquirers wanting heavenly affirmation for their vexing, earthly concerns would line up to have an audience with the priestess-prophetess, a "Pythia," who would go into a trance state from which she would utter the gods' words. Certain rules applied to visitors to the prophetic shrines.

# In the Footsteps of the Rabbi from Tarsus

An inscription at the temple of Athena at Pergamum read: "Whoever wishes to visit the temple of the goddess...must refrain from intercourse with his wife (or husband) that day, [and/or] from intercourse with another than his wife (or husband) for the preceding two days." The temple deity apparently wasn't concerned with folk having sexual liaisons outside of marriage—for this activity was not uncommon even among the gods—and their having sex with "another," be it a male or female, was likewise okay, in marked contrast to Judaism. Temporary sexual restraint seemed to be imposed only for purposes of ritual purification: it is thus related to the "rite" and not to what is "right." Worth noting for our purposes (and Paul's) is the fact that Romans correlated sexual abstinence with divinely inspired prophetic unction: the prophetess herself, remember, was a full-time celibate; and her petitioners were required to embrace restraint on a part-time basis. Might these insights contribute toward our understanding of Paul's discussions on human sexuality in some of his correspondences? As with the tendencies prevailing in the culture, some of his religious hearers seemed bent on sexual denial, whereas others seemed bent on sexual indulgence—both impulses of which can be found in Greco-Roman religious experience.[2]

---

[2] Much as conduct at the sacred shrines was regulated, so too was clothing. For example, a woman was to wear her hair loose when she visited the temple, and a man was to uncover his head. Could these requirements contribute toward our understanding of Paul's notions related to women's hair being covered in 1 Corinthians 11:5-6? This and other questions will be considered later. Let it suffice at this

## Healing Cults in Roman Culture
### *Asclepius*

The popularity of prophetic oracular shrines attests both to the desperate need of people to secure heaven's answers for worldly challenges, and to the perception among the pagans that they actually could get heavenly help, and that they could get it without a commitment to personal holiness. Supernatural "assistance" also applied to bodily healing, said to be a related benefit of sacred shrine prophecy. In fact, various healing cults were known in antiquity, the most prominent of which was the "Cult of Asclepius."

Asclepius, known as a "divine child," was the most human-loving of all the various gods and semi-gods. Born from the union of the god Apollo and Coronis, a mortal woman, Asclepius chose to live on Earth and did not frequent Olympus with the divines. According to his legend, he healed the Earth's sick and even raised the dead. He died and rose from his grave, from which he went on to attend to his primary purpose: health. His daughter "Hygieia" lends moderns the word "hygiene"—which denotes good health. Apollo's famous son Asclepius became the patron god of physicians; the symbol of his walking stick with a serpent intertwined around it has even become the symbol of the American Medical Association. Might Jesus have been casually referring to this image when noting a serpent in the wilderness serving as a remedy for sickness and sin in John 3:14 (cf. Numbers 21:8 [cf.=*compare with*])?

---

juncture to note that Romans followed various religious rules, being anxious to secure the favors of their various gods.

# In the Footsteps of the Rabbi from Tarsus

## Ecstatic Cults in Roman Culture
### *Dionysus*

What Asclepius' relationship was to Apollo, Dionysus' was to Zeus. For as Apollo copulated with a mortal who bore Asclepius, so Zeus engaged in carnal pleasures with a mortal named Semele, who bore him Dionysus—and what a splash Dionysus made! Hera, Zeus' legitimate wife, was incensed! Not to be outdone by a rival, and a mortal one at that, Hera had Semele killed, an act that only led to the immortalization of the child consummated from the illegitimate union. After growing to maturity, the boy-god Dionysus eventually descended to Hades and rescued his mother from the underworld. What a son he was! The joy of the occasion was celebrated with wine— said to be a gift from Dionysus himself.

The adoration of the wine god Dionysus (Bacchus to the Romans) was filled with mystical and emotive celebrations. Celebrants employed wild and ecstatic swirling and dancing to work themselves into frenzied states of emotional and intellectual delirium. At first, devotion to Dionysus primarily appealed to women; in time, however, even men joined the cult.

Why the religious abandon? What was the appeal? If "a picture is worth a thousand words," one might consider artwork from the era as a window into the widespread cult. A fresco outside Pompeii gives us just such a perspective. It shows a woman defending herself from a powerful, demonic, female figure named "Dike"—the mythological "goddess of justice." Though the woman is already

32

beaten, "Dike" strikes her victim over and again. She is subjected to incessant abuse, but she is finally spared the painful experience of relentless judgment. When she is released, the victim, almost entirely naked at this juncture, leaps up and swirls about in reckless abandon—an ecstatic response seen as the supposed depiction of a joyous and blissful afterlife, free of all judgment.

## *Atargatis*

Bizarre as this story is, the power of frenzy is more amply attested in the adoration of the goddess Atargatis of Hierapolis.

Wandering priests devoted to the goddess Atargatis went about advocating for her cult, and their religious adoration was attended by strange practices—the sort that dwarf human imagination. A donkey carried an image of Atargatis in procession, while priests moving about in proximity to her image confessed their sins and beat themselves with whips until their blood flowed freely. They danced about in an intoxicated and frenzied state, playing musical instruments all the while. Wanting to secure alms from among the sympathetic onlookers who were attracted to the odd events, the priests took up financial offerings. But in fact, the small sums they collected were nothing compared to that which sometimes followed, which we'll look at now.

In his *The Syrian Goddess*, Lucian of Samosata wrote that against the backdrop of the loud music and frenzied dance noted above, male priestly candidates would strip off their clothing, grab swords, and castrate themselves.

# In the Footsteps of the Rabbi from Tarsus

Then they would run through the city and throw their disconnected organs into a stranger's home, in response to which they would be granted entrance to the domicile, where they would grab a woman's garment, which would become their new priestly robe. In this way, priests joined themselves to the cult of the goddess and wore women's clothing thereafter.

The popularization of celibacy for priestesses, of ritual castration among priests, of self-mutilated eunuchs parading about in women's apparel, of naked women sensually dancing about in reckless spiritual abandon, all indicate the marriage between supernatural belief and the bizarre. Judaism, for its part, knew none of this and condemned it all outright. These and other practices, however, were standard fare in Roman culture. Mindful of the above, can we wonder that Paul addressed issues related to gender and role confusion and to sexual confusion generally, in his various epistles? Readers cannot understand Paul without understanding his context.

## Sexual Impropriety in Roman Culture

Old Testament Jewish religion defined legitimate sexual practices and the context within which they could be joyfully experienced: marriage. Judaism eschewed certain other practices: homosexuality, for example. Though same-sex acts receive scant attention in the Old Testament, their omission is not tacit consent, but rather because the practice had already been universally condemned among Torah-informed Hebrews. The few places that do mention homosexual practice denounce it outright. Leviticus

18:22 refers to homosexuality as an "abomination," a notion corroborated in 20:13 where Moses stated: "they shall surely be put to death." Without a doubt, homosexuality was given no legitimate place in ancient Israelite culture!

In the New Testament, Paul took issue with immorality in general, as we shall see, and made homosexuality the particular object of his attention at times. In Romans 1:26-27, 1 Corinthians 6:9-10, and 1 Timothy 1:9-10, Paul, like Moses, cast aspersions upon this and other unnatural and morally bankrupt practices.

In his first letter to Timothy, Paul spoke of "lawless" persons as being "insubordinate," "sinners," "unholy," "murderers," "fornicators," "*sodomites,*" and more (1:9-10). Paul had previously written the Corinthians and said as much: "neither fornicators, nor idolaters, nor adulterers, nor *homosexuals,* nor *sodomites*... will inherit the kingdom of God" (1 Corinthians 6:9-10). Paul advocated that Believers keep their impulses bridled within legitimate, sanctioned confines. For statements like these and others, Paul was probably considered way too narrow for the tastes of his Roman contemporaries, many of whom did not share his narrow views. Unbridled sexuality, in all its forms, was everywhere among the ancient Romans— gods and mortals, men and women. Homosexuality was quite common in ancient Greek and Roman societies—an indication of the widespread moral bankruptcy endemic in the culture. The Greek "wise" considered homosexuality a noble and legitimate expression of friendship between men—the highest, in fact. It was so common in Greek academies that same-sex unions between males were referred to as "platonic relationships"—a connection to the academy, where Plato was once a dominant figure. Men sired their legitimate heirs through wives. Mistresses were acceptable for their wandering pleasures, and male lovers of all ages, for purposes of experimentation, were sanctioned too. Roman culture largely accepted this unbridled, licentious activity (as does our own). Even the emperor flaunted it at society's highest levels.

The first-century writer Dio Chrysostom wrote in his 21st Discourse that in 67AD, following the death of his second wife, Poppaea Sabina, the Emperor Nero had his homosexual lover Sporus castrated, gave him the deceased wife's name, "Sabina," and then publicly married him—her!? Writing to the church at Rome approximately ten years before Nero castrated Sporus, Paul opened with a stinging and descriptive condemnation of homosexuality and its uncritical acceptance in Roman society. The *"wrath of God is revealed from heaven against all ungodliness,"* Paul told the Romans in 1:18, and followed with an explication of God's judgment: *"God also gave them over to uncleanness, in the lusts of their hearts, to dishonor their bodies among themselves... God gave them over to vile passions. For even their women exchanged the natural use for what is against nature. Likewise the men, leaving the natural use of the woman, burned in their lust for one another, men with men, committing what is shameful, and receiving in themselves the penalty for the error which was due"* (1:24-27). Paul opposed the rank perfidy in no uncertain terms.

# Paul's Perplexing World

Paul's perspective on the issue of sexual promiscuity—and on other issues—relates squarely to his Jewish origin. In Romans, however, Paul did not condemn the practice on the basis of its being a violation of biblical/Levitical standards, though it clearly violated Judaism's law; rather, he articulated his moral position on the basis that sexual promiscuity was contrary to nature, and to good common sense. Pagans, of course, did not "buy into" Judaism's Bible, and they had no authoritative literature to either quote or argue with, so there was no point in Paul's quoting Scripture to make his point. Besides, pagan mythic gods and heroes engaged in various sexual improprieties and weren't the least bit troubled by same-sex unions. Hedonism—the love of pleasure, including all its queer forms—was modeled for pagans; and for this they can thank their religious guides.

Non-Jews desperately needed to know the Bible! How else could they be grafted into the tree of sanctioned religion and moral practice? Though many of Paul's Jewish contemporaries tended to simply decry the practices of the pagans, and then righteously condemn the pagans themselves in the name of religious indignation, Paul wanted to reach these people who were in desperate need of moral guidance.

The disparaging comment in the Gospel of John that "those who do not know the law are accursed" (7:49) was undisputed among many Judeans in Paul's day. They believed that those who lived outside biblical influence—in other words, the people who lived in the world where

# In the Footsteps of the Rabbi from Tarsus

Paul lived and eventually took Jesus' message—were cursed by their lack of biblical faith, virtue, and revelation. This was particularly true of the licentious Greek and Roman cultures, far removed from biblical real estate and the biblical influences that held sway in Jerusalem and Judea.

Though Greek thought and practices made inroads into Judaic culture in the Greco-Roman era, the lines dividing Hebraic and Hellenistic visions and virtues were still clear to many. Sexual impropriety, which was eschewed in Judaism, was rife in ancient non-Jewish philosophy and practice. Without moral rules of engagement, powerful Greeks and Romans gave no thought to sexually molesting their powerless slaves, seeing them as little more than their "living property" and thus as instruments and utilities to be used as they, their rightful owners, saw fit. In like manner, young boys were granted no protective sanctuary from the sexual advances and exploitive interests of immoral older boys and adult males or females. Even the tolerance of crucifixion as a means of execution demonstrates the horrific wickedness and brutality of the times, and indicates how public policy was shaped by unscrupulous, value-impoverished individuals. Add the numerous public bathhouses, the Greek habit of conducting athletic competitions in the nude, and the grotesque gladiatorial games celebrated in Rome and elsewhere, and *a picture of a culture without a strong moral compass clearly emerges.* Against this backdrop, the Judeans' nervousness in approaching the gentile culture is entirely understandable, and perhaps commendable.

# Paul's Perplexing World

Without a moral compass, Greco-Roman gentiles were oriented differently than were many Jews in the Greco-Roman world. Individual Jews might not have followed all of the Torah's particulars, but at least the Jews had the Scriptures and knew there was a moral standard. Non-Jews, on the other hand, had no culture-wide standard to decry the aforementioned, "accursed" practices. Sin was life in Greco-Roman culture!

New Testament readers have long noted that early Believers in Jesus had trouble dealing with the non-Jewish culture and all its practices. Jesus' disciples, for example, marveled that Jesus would converse with an immoral Samaritan woman in John 4:27; for they did not expect their rabbi to converse with "those people"—non-Jewish outsiders. Peter's flagrant withdrawal from table talk with gentiles in Galatia drew a criticism from Paul in Galatians 2:11-13, where Paul said, "I withstood him to his face" for his insincerity. Peter had a real problem—as did other Jews: *How would Jews come to terms with non-Jews and their non-Jewish culture, given what Jews knew about that culture?* Paul had some ideas; and those ideas—though not entirely his—are reflected in his writings.

As noted at this chapter's outset, for the Jews, the Law (the Torah) was a standard, a schoolmaster informing individuals how to walk in God's will, and how they could better know His ways. How would non-Jews who received Israel's "Messiah" learn to walk uprightly when they were unfamiliar with Israel's Scriptures? Paul answered by listing *vices* and *virtues*. Though sympathetic and personally connected to Jewish practice, *Paul never required that non-Jews embrace the ritual forms of Judaism; he did, however, believe it was necessary for them to adhere to the Torah's moral principles.* The Messianic Rabbi from Tarsus taught Torah virtues to non-Jews—moral principles taken from ancient Jewish literature, articulated with contemporary Hebraic thoughts, and contextualized for his non-Jewish hearers.

Paul never tired of putting the "new law" in front of his audiences. Paul's "new way" was, in a sense, a Messianic vision from the "old way." Paul still advocated for Jewish biblical values and practices, which he reframed and rearticulated for his non-Jewish followers. For example, instead of Judaism versus non-Judaism, Paul spoke of the "spirit" versus the "flesh"—a framework akin to Judaism's "good inclination" and "evil inclination." To Paul, it was important that Believers live rightly—in the Spirit. Paul felt that ritual religion—in all its forms—had a limited ability to affect and ameliorate the human condition, with its innate tendency toward sinfulness.

Ritual religion did not provide practicing Jews and morally inclined gentiles the much-needed change of heart; nor could pagans lost in Greek mythologies find salvation, or get the necessary moral guidance. In Colossians 2:20-22, Paul challenged his readers, rhetorically asking: "Why do you subject yourself to regulations—do not touch, do not taste, do not handle... according to the commandments of doctrines of men?" "These things," said he in v. 23, "have an appearance of wisdom in self-imposed religion, false humility, and neglect of the body, but are of no value against the indulgence of the flesh." For Paul, the real spiritual battle was fought internally; and external practices, though perhaps good in and of themselves, did little to purchase the power necessary to overcome the inhospitable evil forces that beset humankind.

If ritualized religion could not change the human condition, what could? Receive the "spirit" and "walk in the spirit," said Paul to the Galatians; then "do not gratify the desires of the flesh" (5:16). So as not to leave his new converts in the dark on the meaning of this dichotomy, he detailed what he meant by vice and virtue—and he repeated this elsewhere.

In Galatians 5:19-21, Paul said "The works of the flesh are evident, which are: adultery, fornication, uncleanness, lewdness, idolatry, sorcery, hatred, contentions, jealousies, outbursts of wrath, selfish ambitions, dissensions, heresies, envy, murders, drunkenness, revelries and the like; of which I tell you beforehand, just as I told you in time past, that those who practice such things will not inherit the kingdom of God." The seventeen particular vices listed here were all deemed destructive. His mention that the list of vices was shared with them in a "time past" probably harks back to an oral teaching, given that his letter to the Galatians is one of Paul's earliest writings, if not the first one. Clearly, the "works of the flesh" were understood to be morally reprehensible; but, as I noted before, not because they violated the Mosaic economy—though they clearly ran counter to the Torah's teachings.

Rather, the practices were eschewed as a defiance of virtue-based living.

Immediately after listing the carnal vices, Paul delineated examples of virtue-based, or Spirit-led living: "But, the fruit of the Spirit is love, joy, peace, longsuffering, kindness, goodness, faithfulness, gentleness, self control. Against such there is no law" (vv. 22-23). The imposition of standards was not far from his thinking, as evidenced by his internal response to his own statement, "against such there is no law."

To be sure, Paul did not foist Jewish ceremonial law on his non-Jewish congregants. He did, however, advocate for the morally rich principles of Judaism, which were delineated from the Jewish Scriptures. He wanted his non-Jewish flock to embrace these "old" standards and carry them in the "new lives" they were "born again" into. Paul wanted to help people clean themselves up. Just as Jews designate "kosher" (clean) and "unkosher" (unclean), Paul repackaged Old Testament notions of what was clean and acceptable and presented them in a new, Messiah-centered framework, emphasizing the unclean habits of the "flesh" and the right ways of the "spirit." This he did while exhorting folk to "walk in spirit and not satisfy the desires of the flesh."

How Paul accomplished this is the subject of the next chapter where we begin our exploration of his actions by listening to his biographer, Luke. After hearing Luke tell of Paul's travels, and to a certain extent his teachings,

# Paul's Perplexing World

we'll hear Paul firsthand by surveying the rabbi's writings and considering some of the principal and principled teachings he offered in his epistles.

As we move on to examine Paul's actions, let's remember the morally rudderless world that Paul called home and appreciate why Paul wanted to bring biblical perspective to relieve individuals' assorted human hurts. Let's also marvel at how the Rabbi from Tarsus was a worldwide rabbi, given that he meant to engage the entire world with Israel's Hope and Scriptures.

# II

## The *Acts* of the Apostle Paul

### Introduction

As noted at the outset, this book is primarily concerned with Paul's *movements* and *parchments.* Besides Paul's own occasional and brief reference to his movements, the only credible source for Paul's travels is the writings of his biographer, Luke, in the New Testament. We will present a brief introduction to Paul's emerging as the New Testament's principal "mover," "shaker," and "writer" through the writings of Luke. Through this, readers will be

# In the Footsteps of the Rabbi from Tarsus

better able to come to terms with the famous and controversial Rabbi from Tarsus—Paul.

## Emergence of the Messianic Rabbi from Tarsus

Luke's report of Paul's travels is found in a New Testament book inaccurately called the "Acts of the Apostles," or simply "Acts." This title is not taken from the Text itself, but is imposed by tradition. Frankly, it would be nice to have a real book that lives up to that name—something about the Apostles' actual acts. But we have nothing close to that in the biblical writings.

In the so-called "Acts of the Apostles," the Apostles are mentioned as a group only once (in 1:15-26), and then only in passing. After Judas' betrayal and subsequent suicide, Luke says that there was a need to find an apostolic replacement to keep the number of Apostles at an even twelve—comparable to there being twelve patriarchs, twelve tribes, etc. After this, the apostolic community vanishes from the book entirely—evidence enough that the book really isn't about the "Apostles," collectively, at all.

In Acts, the most prominence is initially given to one Apostle, Peter, but he fades away quickly. The real object of Luke's attention then surfaces: *telling of the activities and, to a lesser extent, the teachings of a man named Paul.* Through a strange turn of events, he became something of an honorary Apostle and the Church's principal congregational planter and its most enduring theologian.

# The *Acts* of the Apostle Paul

Instead of "Acts of the Apostles," A title truer to the intention of the author would be "Acts of the *Apostle Paul*." Luke is our go-to source for a formal journal of the footsteps of this Rabbi from Tarsus and we turn to his writings now.

As Luke begins his book of "Acts," he mentions a "former account," which he recommended to a patron of his named "Theophilus" (Acts 1:1). This "account," known formally to us as "The Gospel According to Luke," begins with a notation to this same Theophilus (cf. Lk. 1:3). From this we can conclude that Luke first wrote an official and orderly accounting of Jesus' life in the Gospel of Luke, and followed it with another accounting, this time of the movement's growth in the wake of its Founder's crucifixion.

In this second volume—what has been incorrectly called "Acts of the Apostles"—Luke tells about Peter and then concentrates on the rise of the movement's effective new advocate, Paul. The New Testament's principal historian, Luke—who, by the way, was also the associate of the New Testament's principal theologian, Paul—gives an orderly account of the Messianic Jesus movement's beginnings in Judea, and tells of its advancement to places beyond, what Jesus prophetically called "the uttermost parts of the Earth" (1:8). A brief examination of how this happened follows.

47

# In the Footsteps of the Rabbi from Tarsus

## Overview of Luke's Pauline Texts

Theologians universally consider Acts 1:8 as the passage that sets the book's theme and tone. After "receiving power when the Holy Spirit has come" upon them, the early disciples were commanded by Jesus to be "witnesses to Me in Jerusalem, and in all Judea and Samaria, and to the end of the Earth." Fulfilling Jesus' instruction, Luke tells of the fledgling movement, and in chapter 9 introduces its main advocate and the Church's most significant theologian—Rabbi Paul. Luke's historical narrative tells of the movement's advancement, paying attention to how the Gospel spread and penetrated into new worlds beyond its Founder's host culture in Judea.

Luke notes that, in the wake of the incredible outpouring of the Spirit, the fledgling movement progressed significantly: "So continuing daily with one accord in the temple, and breaking bread from house to house, they ate their food with gladness and simplicity of heart, praising God and having favor with all the people. And the Lord added to the church daily those who were being saved" (2:46-47).

Professor Stanley D. Toussaint of the Dallas Theological Seminary observes in the Text what he refers to as "progress reports" that underscore the movement's successes and its outward-moving penetration into new cultures. Dr. Toussaint suggests that these "reports" are keys to unlocking the book's outline. The optimistic assessment in 2:46-47 is considered to be the first of seven examples where Luke intersperses his historical accounting with various summaries and upbeat assessments.

# The *Acts* of the Apostle Paul

For example, after reporting the Gospel's expansion in Jerusalem in 3:1-6:6, Luke gives a word of encouragement in 6:7—a progress report: "Then the word of God spread, and the number of the disciples multiplied greatly in Jerusalem, and a great many of the priests were obedient to the faith." Luke testifies about the Spirit mobilizing an expanding enterprise, with Peter initially as the Lord's foremost vessel. In addition, Luke informs that the advancement does not go uncontested, and says that Paul plays a part in its setback.

In chapter six, Luke introduces Stephen's boundless faith and vitality, describing him as "full of faith and power" (v. 8). Luke reports at length how Stephen's passion invoked the outrage of the powers that be, with the result that he was arrested and subsequently maligned (6:8-7:1). Not the least bit dissuaded by his unfortunate turn of circumstances, Stephen spoke boldly to his accusers (vv. 2-53), which swiftly brought about his tragic stoning (vv. 54-60). In 7:54-58, Stephen's unwarranted and cruel death is inextricably linked to one named Saul—later called Paul, who becomes "The Rabbi from Tarsus." At this juncture, however, he was probably more accurately described by the Believers as the "Rabbi from Hell."

Luke describes Stephen's savage death: an unruly "crowd ran at him with one accord; and they cast him out of the city and stoned him" and they "laid down their clothes at the feet of a young man named Saul" (v. 58b). Thus, the

In the Footsteps of the Rabbi from Tarsus

book's soon-to-be heroic figure, Saul/Paul, is first represented as supporting a vicious murder.

After reporting the death of Stephen, Luke introduces another character, Philip. Luke emphasizes Philip's bent on preaching the Gospel *beyond* Israel—in Samaria and to an Ethiopian (8:5-40). The Gospel is represented as advancing, but not to the "uttermost parts of the earth"— at least, not yet.

Luke tells of Saul's spectacular "conversion" (chapter 9), played out against the backdrop of specific and general persecutions of the fledgling Messianic Jewish movement (8:1). After this Saul (our Paul) was miraculously transformed on the road to Damascus, a relative calm descended over the Church which, prior to this, was experiencing trying times. Luke's third victory report follows in 9:31: "Then the churches throughout all Judea, Galilee, and Samaria had peace and were edified. And walking in the fear of the Lord and in the comfort of the Holy Spirit, they were multiplied."

In 9:32-35, Luke tells of the Gospel's expansion beyond Judea. In 11:19-30 readers are informed how the movement expanded into Antioch, "where the disciples were first called Christians" (11:26). Luke then draws attention to more precarious affairs in Jerusalem, where the church in Antioch marshaled resources to give aid (11:29-30), which was sent to Jerusalem "by the hands of Barnabas and Saul" (v. 30). After describing the rising misery index among the brethren in Judea (12:1-23),

# The *Acts* of the Apostle Paul

Luke gives his fourth progress report: "But the word of God grew and multiplied" (v. 24), and follows with Barnabas and Paul's return to Antioch from Jerusalem, with John Mark in tow (v. 25).

Meanwhile back in Antioch, this cosmopolitan congregation's missionary spirit became overpowering (13:1-2), with the result that Paul and Barnabas were selected to serve as their official missionary advocates (v. 3). Luke gives an abbreviated account of their first circuit tour in Asia Minor (modern Islamic Turkey) in chapters 13-14, but interestingly spends more time detailing a follow-up conference in Acts 15 over misunderstandings about the nature of Paul's ministry—problems which arose because of Paul's non-conventional gentile mission. After a rather engaging church conference (vv. 1-21) characterized by spirited arguments over Paul's bold initiatives, Paul was officially approved (vv. 22-24). Luke gives the fifth progress report, saying that "the churches were strengthened in the faith and increased in number daily" (16:5). Paul went off again to advance the Messianic Kingdom beyond Israel's borders (16:6-21:15)—with unswerving and unbounded zeal. His enthusiasm was, no doubt, encouraged by the endorsement he'd received in Jerusalem.

Believing himself to be under a Divine mandate to press on, Paul opted to forgo his overland travels and press eastward to Greece by sea (16:9-10). He sailed from Troas (v. 11) and made his way to Philippi (v. 12), where his message was contested, but eventually received (vv. 13-40).

# In the Footsteps of the Rabbi from Tarsus

On the Greek mainland, Paul made his way west by southwest, reaching Amphipolis, Appolonia, Thessalonica, Berea, and elsewhere (17:1). With roots eventually established in Macedonia (northern Greece), the intrepid apostolic explorer ventured farther southward down the Grecian peninsula to Athens (in southern Greece) (v. 15). After a sojourn there, he made his way to Corinth (18:1). His second missionary journey at an end (vv. 19-22), Paul departed that region for his home base in Antioch.

After a season of refreshment in Antioch, Paul took off again (18:23) on what scholars call his "third missionary journey." Luke gives particular attention to events in Ephesus (19:1-41), where a riot broke out, provoked by angry idol-makers concerned by a drop in revenue caused by the Jesus movement's growth. Amidst the turbulence, God's grace was manifest still. Difficulties aside, Luke gives his sixth progress report: "the word of the Lord grew mightily and prevailed" (v. 20). When "the uproar had ceased," Paul departed for Greece again (20:1-2). He conducted and completed his third journey, and then went to Jerusalem where he was arrested and held on spurious charges (21:33). From there, he went to Caesarea where he was confined (23:33), after which he was sent to Rome for trial, as a result of his appeal (25:10-11). Luke finishes the book telling of Paul's acts, and concludes with a final progress report—his seventh—noting that the Word was still going forth unhindered: "Paul dwelt two whole years in his own rented house [in Rome], and received all who came to him, preaching the kingdom of God and teaching the things which concern

# The *Acts* of the Apostle Paul

the Lord Jesus Christ with all confidence, no one forbidding him" (28:30-31).

## Paul's Conversion and Preparation          *Acts 9-12*

Having offered an overview of Paul's *acts* in Acts, we will now look more closely at the *facts* in Acts, by examining the book's particulars, noting Paul's significance in the volume.

Luke says that Paul's entrance into the Church's post-Jesus ministry story came on the heels of a Jewish evangelist and apologist named Stephen, who invoked the ire of frenzied, anti-Messianic Jews, who then mercilessly fell upon him and slew him. Paul was more than a casual observer to this activity, and was regarded as being instrumental in encouraging the event. In 7:57-60 readers are told: "then they cried out with a loud voice, stopped their ears, and ran at him [Stephen] with one accord; and they cast him out of the city and stoned him. *And the witnesses laid down their clothes at the feet of a young man named Saul.* And they stoned Stephen as he was calling on God and saying, 'Lord Jesus, receive my spirit.' Then he knelt down and cried out with a loud voice, 'Lord, do not charge them with this sin.' And when he had said this, he fell asleep."

*As Stephen fell "asleep," one wonders if something was beginning to awaken in Paul.* If something was, the actual dawning of Paul's new day was still further away. Luke notes that Paul was hell-bent on wreaking havoc—and more was to come.

# In the Footsteps of the Rabbi from Tarsus

After noting the grace with which Stephen accepted his fate, Luke says that Saul more than casually approved of their actions and that he was not satisfied with this one casualty, but wanted to attack and eradicate the entire group.

In 8:1 we're told, "Now Saul was consenting to his death," and Luke describes what happened while Paul worked to end the Messianic movement. In 9:1-2, Luke says: "Then Saul, still breathing threats and murder against the disciples of the Lord, went to the high priest and asked letters from him to the synagogues of Damascus, so that if he found any who were of the Way, whether men or women, he might bring them bound to Jerusalem." Then we're told, "As he journeyed he came near Damascus, and suddenly a light shone around him from heaven. Then he fell to the ground, and heard a voice saying to him, 'Saul, Saul, why are you persecuting Me?'" By way of response, in v. 5 he went on: "And he said, 'Who are You, Lord?' Then the Lord said, 'I am Jesus, whom you are persecuting. It is hard for you to kick against the goads'" (vv. 3-4).

Paul was knocked off his horse by the ordeal. Luke continues:

> 9:6 So he, trembling and astonished, said, "Lord, what do You want me to do?" Then the Lord said to him, "Arise and go into the city, and you will be told what you must do."

# The *Acts* of the Apostle Paul

7 And the men who journeyed with him stood speechless, hearing a voice but seeing no one. 8 Then Saul arose from the ground, and when his eyes were opened he saw no one. But they led him by the hand and brought him into Damascus. 9 And he was three days without sight, and neither ate nor drank."

By now, Paul's reputation as an anti-Messianic hellraiser was apparently firmly established, with the net result that the brethren did not want to approach him—even after word of his conversion. Luke continues:

9:10 Now there was a certain disciple at Damascus named Ananias; and to him the Lord said in a vision, "Ananias." And he said, "Here I am, Lord." 11 So the Lord said to him, "Arise and go to the street called Straight, and inquire at the house of Judas for one called Saul of Tarsus, for behold, he is praying. 12 And in a vision he has seen a man named Ananias coming in and putting his hand on him, so that he might receive his sight." 13 Then Ananias answered, "Lord, I have heard from many about this man, how much harm he has done to Your saints in Jerusalem. 14 And here he has authority from the chief priests to bind all who call on Your name."

15 But the Lord said to him, "Go, for he is a chosen vessel of Mine to bear My name before Gentiles, kings, and the children of Israel. 16 For I will show

him how many things he must suffer for My name's sake."

Ananias went and ministered to Paul, over his own understandable objections, and the rest is history. Would that we all compliantly heeded God's callings, even when we're asked to contradict our shortsighted judgments! The narrative picks up:

> 9:17 And Ananias went his way and entered the house; and laying his hands on him he said, "Brother Saul, the Lord Jesus, who appeared to you on the road as you came, has sent me that you may receive your sight and be filled with the Holy Spirit." 18 Immediately there fell from his eyes something like scales, and he received his sight at once; and he arose and was baptized. 19 So when he had received food, he was strengthened. Then Saul spent some days with the disciples at Damascus.

It seems that the Believers came to terms with the reality of Paul's transformative experience, though they were nervous at first.

It is worth being reminded at this juncture that Paul was *not* an original Apostle. Not only was he not part of the first group but, even after joining the movement in spirit, he didn't go to Jerusalem to confer with them. He went to Syria instead! *Interestingly, Paul was "converted" into the movement, without having firsthand knowledge of what it was all about.* Though "converted," he wasn't converted from Judaism—for he lived as a Jew till his dying day. He was a converted sinner in possession of a new nature! Transformed now, this rabbi was a Spirit-led vessel through whom God could advance His Kingdom's purposes. Paul showed signs of his calling shortly after his conversion.

> 9:20 Immediately he [Paul] preached the Christ in the synagogues, that He is the Son of God. 21 Then all who heard were amazed, and said, "Is this not he who destroyed those who called on this name in Jerusalem, and has come here for that purpose, so that he might bring them bound to the chief priests?"

In v. 22 we're told, "Saul increased all the more in strength, and confounded the Jews who dwelt in Damascus, proving that this Jesus is the Christ [the Messiah]."

What was the upshot of his ministry? He who rejected the Church was himself rejected. He who inflicted miseries bore many himself. Personal tragedy was to follow him his entire apostolic career, but he seemed to bear it with grace.

Though Jesus said that "the gates of hell will not *prevail*," He never promised that the gates of hell would not *assail.* Evidence of the latter is taken from the following:

> 9:23 Now after many days were past, the Jews plotted to kill him. 24 But their plot became known to Saul. And they watched the gates day

and night, to kill him. 25 Then the disciples took him by night and let him down through the wall in a large basket.

He escaped! They were on to him, and the pressure was never to let up—never.

Given his reputation as a former persecutor of the Church, Believers remained afraid of him for quite some time. The situation began to change, however, when a man of repute named Barnabas took Paul under his wing and afforded him the opportunity to develop some credibility. We're told:

> 9:26 And when Saul had come to Jerusalem, he tried to join the disciples; but they were all afraid of him, and did not believe that he was a disciple. 27 But Barnabas took him and brought him to the apostles. And he declared to them how he had seen the Lord on the road, and that He had spoken to him, and how he had preached boldly at Damascus in the name of Jesus.
>
> 28 So he was with them at Jerusalem, coming in and going out. 29 And he spoke boldly in the name of the Lord Jesus and disputed against the Hellenists, but they attempted to kill him. 30 When the brethren found out, they brought him down to Caesarea and sent him out to Tarsus.

# The *Acts* of the Apostle Paul

As noted in the introduction, Luke finishes in v. 31 with a progress report: "Then the churches throughout all Judea, Galilee, and Samaria had peace and were edified. And walking in the fear of the Lord and in the comfort of the Holy Spirit, they were multiplied."

Luke then shifts gears and focuses on Peter, not Paul (9:32-11:18). The importance of his doing this cannot be overstated! Let's see why.

Spirited along by a heavenly vision, and beckoned by a non-Jew named Cornelius (10:1-33), a reluctant Peter sheepishly went to minister to this receptive gentile, who subsequently had his own Pentecost experience (10:44-48). After his first gentile conversion, Peter was called on to explain this odd turn of events to the Jewish brethren (11:1-18). The result was that—though uncomfortable at first with extending their message to gentiles—they accepted this new happening. Luke notes: "When they heard these things they became silent; and they glorified God, saying, *'Then God has also granted to the Gentiles repentance to life'* (v. 18). Luke underscores that Peter was the *first* to minister to gentiles, and that the activity was given an apostolic seal of approval. Luke then shifts to Paul, who more than anyone, will go on and do what *Peter did first: minister to non-Jews.* The point is that the precedent was set before Paul's arrival.

Now, Luke returns to Paul's story, which he'd interrupted:

> 11:19 Now those who were scattered after the persecution that arose over Stephen traveled as far as Phoenicia, Cyprus, and Antioch, preaching the word to no one but the Jews only. 20 But some of them were men from Cyprus and Cyrene, who, when they had come to Antioch, spoke to the Hellenists, preaching the Lord Jesus. 21 And the hand of the Lord was with them, and a great number believed and turned to the Lord.

With news of the revival and expansion of the Gospel, readers are told:

> 11:22 Then news of these things came to the ears of the church in Jerusalem, and they sent out Barnabas to go as far as Antioch. 23 When he came and had seen the grace of God, he was glad, and encouraged them all that with purpose of heart they should continue with the Lord.

After noting in v. 24 that "a great many [other] people were added to the Lord," Luke says that *"Barnabas departed for Tarsus to seek Saul.* And when he had found him, he brought him to Antioch. So it was that for a whole year they assembled with the church and taught a great many people. And the disciples were first called Christians in Antioch" (25-26).

It seems that Paul was drawn into the apostolic net. What many don't know—or prefer to avoid—is that the man who would later become the "Apostle to the

Gentiles" loved the Jews and cut his teeth on being of service to *them*. Luke continues by underscoring this fact:

> 11:27 And in these days prophets came from Jerusalem to Antioch. 28 Then one of them, named Agabus, stood up and showed by the Spirit that there was going to be a great famine throughout all the world, which also happened in the days of Claudius Caesar. 29 Then the disciples, each according to his ability, determined to send relief to the brethren dwelling in Judea. 30 This they also did, and sent it to the elders by the hands of Barnabas and Saul.

After noting Paul and Barnabas' involvement in helping the fledgling Messianic Jews, Luke tells of the hardships that the Jewish Believers experienced (12:1-4), and then focuses again on Peter's miseries and deliverance (vv. 5-19), before closing with a comment on Herod's demise in vv. 20-23. Luke offers another progress report: "But the word of God grew and multiplied. And Barnabas and Saul returned from Jerusalem when they had fulfilled their ministry, and they also took with them John whose surname was Mark" (vv. 24-25).

## Paul's First Journey, 46-48AD          *Acts 13-14*
We observe no emphasis, whatsoever, on the Apostles collectively in this so-called "Acts of the Apostles." There is some brief mention of Peter—and that's about it; and these few references are offered only to support Paul's

ministry. Through them, Paul's ministry to the gentiles is shown as riding on the heels of Peter's ministry to the gentiles and subsequent authorization. After this, Peter's story fades away. Peter's *decline* in the narrative plays out against the backdrop of Paul's *incline*. Paul's rising career gains authority by this means. In what follows immediately, his being set apart for the ministry is noted—and in a manner that is very telling.

Chapter 13 begins:

> 13:1 Now in the church that was at Antioch there were certain prophets and teachers: Barnabas, Simeon who was called Niger, Lucius of Cyrene, Manaen who had been brought up with Herod the tetrarch, and Saul. 2 As they ministered to the Lord and fasted, the Holy Spirit said, "Now separate to Me Barnabas and Saul for the work to which I have called them." 3 Then, having fasted and prayed, and laid hands on them, they sent them away.

A quick look at the church that sent Paul shows the following. First, the cosmopolitan congregation in Antioch was made up of a diverse band of leaders. Barnabas was from Cyprus (see Acts 4:36). Simeon is called "Niger" (meaning a "black" man), and Lucius is from Cyrene, a city in northern Africa. Various ethnic groups are represented in the church at Antioch. In addition, Manaen was "brought up with Herod," indicating that he enjoyed status and privilege. It seems that the church there had penetrated into different social groups, not just ethnic ones.

# The *Acts* of the Apostle Paul

Once dispatched, Paul and company set their sights westward: "So, being sent out by the Holy Spirit, they went down to Seleucia, and from there they sailed to Cyprus. And when they arrived in Salamis, they preached the word of God in the synagogues of the Jews. They also had John as their assistant" (13:4-5)—an arrangement that would soon be undone, due to Mark's untimely wavering. In any case…

> 13:6 Now when they had gone through the island to Paphos, they found a certain sorcerer, a false prophet, a Jew whose name was Bar-Jesus, 7 who was with the proconsul, Sergius Paulus, an intelligent man. This man called for Barnabas and Saul and sought to hear the word of God. 8 But Elymas the sorcerer (for so his name is translated) withstood them, seeking to turn the proconsul away from the faith. 9 Then Saul, who also is called Paul, filled with the Holy Spirit, looked intently at him 10 and said, "O full of all deceit and all fraud, you son of the devil, you enemy of all right-eousness, will you not cease perverting the straight ways of the Lord? 11 And now, indeed, the hand of the Lord is upon you, and you shall be blind, not seeing the sun for a time." And immediately a dark mist fell on him, and he went around seeking someone to lead him by the hand. 12 Then the proconsul believed, when he saw what had been done, being astonished at the teaching of the Lord.

# In the Footsteps of the Rabbi from Tarsus

Through this story, a "full of the Holy Spirit" Paul is bold and forthright, and able to cause afflictions—blindness, in this case—as proof of his spiritual and apostolic authorization.

Continuing in v. 13, Luke says: "Now when Paul and his party set sail from Paphos, they came to Perga in Pamphylia; and John, departing from them, returned to Jerusalem"—a situation that would come back to haunt them later. John Mark probably saw the hazards of the journey and wasn't inclined to press on. It is worth noting that Paul, the "Apostle to the Gentiles," continually met with the Jews—a custom he never deviated from:

> 13:14 But when they departed from Perga, they came to Antioch in Pisidia, and went into the synagogue on the Sabbath day and sat down. 15 And after the reading of the Law and the Prophets, the rulers of the synagogue sent to them, saying, "Men and brethren, if you have any word of exhortation for the people, say on."

Paul was invited to speak because he was a "card-carrying member" of the Pharisees and as such, he was granted privilege as a distinguished theologian. In due time, the local authorities discovered that he wasn't quite what they were expecting and they took exception—but not before Paul got his point across.

In v. 16 we're told: "Then Paul stood up, and motioning with his hand said, 'Men of Israel, and you who fear

# The *Acts* of the Apostle Paul

God, listen...'" He went on to give an address, harking back to the story of Egyptian bondage, the Exodus, and King Saul, David's rise, John the Baptist's ministry, and then Jesus (vv. 17-26). He challenged them to respond to Jesus (vv. 27-37) culminating with this:

> 13:38 "Therefore let it be known to you, brethren, that through this Man is preached to you the forgiveness of sins; 39 and by Him everyone who believes is justified from all things from which you could not be justified by the law of Moses. 40 Beware therefore, lest what has been spoken in the prophets come upon you:
>
> 41 'Behold, you despisers,
> Marvel and perish!
> For I work a work in your days,
> A work which you will by no means believe,
> Though one were to declare it to you'"

Paul's appeal to Old Testament history was followed by a direct appeal, challenge, and warning (from Habakkuk 1:5).

In response to his stirring appeal, "When the Jews went out of the synagogue, the Gentiles begged that these words might be preached to them the next Sabbath." Luke reports "when the congregation had broken up, many of the Jews and devout proselytes followed Paul and Barnabas, who, speaking to them, persuaded them to continue in the grace of God" (v. 43).

# In the Footsteps of the Rabbi from Tarsus

A few things are striking in these exchanges. First, Paul's straightforward manner is noteworthy, especially given how it contrasts to much of the preaching today—which tends to be nice by comparison. That the "Apostle to the Gentiles" is found in the synagogue *first,* is not only shown here, but will become apparent throughout Luke's account of his "acts." Paul's frequenting of synagogues, as was his manner, not only enforces his connection to Judaism, but also supports the case that Paul's gentiles were not gentiles in the classic, non-Jewish or anti-Jewish sense. To the contrary, Paul's gentiles were half-baked Jews—people who were assimilating into Jewish culture. They were Jewish-loving gentiles, whom he encountered in the course of visiting synagogues where they were associating with the Jews, learning the Jewish language, literature, customs, and more.

The Jewish leaders were disconcerted by what they saw as a strange turn of events. Paul was too controversial for them. It was easy to invite him in as he was a Pharisee; but, the next question was not so simple: How can we get him out?

What Luke shares next sets the pattern for Paul's ministry in Acts:

> 13:44 On the next Sabbath almost the whole city came together to hear the word of God. 45 But when the Jews saw the multitudes, they were filled with envy; and contradicting and blaspheming, they opposed the things spoken by Paul. 46 Then

# The *Acts* of the Apostle Paul

Paul and Barnabas grew bold and said, "It was necessary that the word of God should be spoken to you first; but since you reject it, and judge yourselves unworthy of everlasting life, behold, we turn to the Gentiles. 47 For so the Lord has commanded us: 'I have set you as a light to the Gentiles, That you should be for salvation to the ends of the earth.'"

That the "whole city" came together indicates that Paul was very controversial—something of a rabble-rouser. That religious leaders were "jealous" of him, attests to the popularity he enjoyed among their former followers. Paul swayed them in a new direction, angering the religious leaders. Paul's saying that it was necessary to bring the Word to you first; "but since you reject it...we turn to the Gentiles" should not be construed as a change of direction or affection. Some misconstrue this as Paul telling the Jews they no longer matter, that he was now turning to non-Jews. Though understandable at one level— on the basis of this passage alone—the fact that Paul continued to frequent Jewish synagogues and lovingly associate with Jews after this incident implies that this was a local situation. He, in effect, said: "OK, since I no longer am going to having a gentlemanly hearing with my Jewish associates here, I am going to disengage from this synagogue and leave them be." This, as I've said, was driven more by practicality—they didn't want him any longer. It should not be construed as any change of his heart's affection, however, for it was not.

# In the Footsteps of the Rabbi from Tarsus

In any case, Luke goes on in vv. 48-52 to say that "when the Gentiles heard this, they were glad and glorified the word of the Lord. And as many as had been appointed to eternal life believed. And the word of the Lord was being spread throughout all the region. But the Jews stirred up the devout and prominent women and the chief men of the city, raised up persecution against Paul and Barnabas, and expelled them from their region." In response, as Jesus did before him, Paul and company "shook off the dust from their feet against them, and came to Iconium. And the disciples were filled with joy and with the Holy Spirit."

Proof that Paul remained within Judaism is offered in the following passage, where he frequents the synagogue—and garners a supportive hearing from Jews and gentiles alike.

In 14:1, Luke states that while in Iconium "they went together to the synagogue of the Jews, and so spoke that a great multitude both of the Jews and of the Greeks believed." But again, discontent surfaced: "But the unbelieving Jews stirred up the Gentiles and poisoned their minds against the brethren" (v. 2). And so the story repeats… over and over again in Paul's ministry.

Paul apparently understood his struggles as simply the hazards of the profession and was not particularly bothered by them. In v. 3 Luke says that they "stayed there a long time, speaking boldly in the Lord, who was bearing witness to the word of His grace, granting signs and

# The *Acts* of the Apostle Paul

wonders to be done by their hands." Luke notes Paul's tenacity and the fact that his ministry was supported by "signs and wonders."

Still, as happened in every case, "the multitude of the city was divided: part sided with the Jews [who were discontented], and part with the apostles" (v. 4). Luke reports that "a violent attempt was made by both the Gentiles and Jews, with their rulers, to abuse and stone them, [but] they became aware of it and fled to Lystra and Derbe, cities of Lycaonia, and to the surrounding region. And they were preaching the gospel there" (vv. 5-7).

Much as Peter was used to heal a lame fellow previously (see v. 3:1ff), Luke relates that "in Lystra a certain man without strength in his feet was sitting, a cripple from his mother's womb, who had never walked. This man heard Paul speaking. Paul, observing him intently and seeing that he had faith to be healed, said with a loud voice, 'Stand up straight on your feet!,' and he leaped and walked" (vv. 8-10).

Luke writes of miracles, strengthening the notion that Paul was as much an Apostle as Peter, despite Paul's not having been an original disciple of Jesus. The same Spirit at work in Peter ministering to the Jews, was at work in Paul ministering to gentiles—gentiles who followed some, but not all, Jewish customs.

Even the pagans were impressed by the display of miracle-power; for, "when the people saw what Paul had done, they raised their voices, saying in the Lycaonian language, 'The gods have come down to us in the likeness of men!'" (v. 11)

> 14:12 And Barnabas they called Zeus, and Paul, Hermes, because he was the chief speaker. 13 Then, the priest of Zeus, whose temple was in front of their city, brought oxen and garlands to the gates, intending to sacrifice with the multitudes. 14 But when the apostles Barnabas and Paul heard this, they tore their clothes and ran in among the multitude, crying out 15 and saying, "Men, why are you doing these things? We also are men with the same nature as you, and preach to you that you should turn from these useless things to the living God, who made the heaven, the earth, the sea, and all things that are in them, 16 who in bygone generations allowed all nations to walk in their own ways. 17 Nevertheless He did not leave Himself without witness, in that He did good, gave us rain from heaven and fruitful seasons, filling our hearts with food and gladness." 18 And with these sayings they could scarcely restrain the multitudes from sacrificing to them."

Paul's argument is very Jewish. Luke describes him as standing inside of Judaism and rejecting idol-worship. Just because some Jewish officials kicked him out of their synagogue, we mustn't make the mistake of thinking that Paul left his beloved Jewish universe. He argues for

# The *Acts* of the Apostle Paul

principles sacred to Judaism when speaking with the non-Jewish cultures.

Despite these displays of affection, "Jews from Antioch and Iconium came there; and having persuaded the multitudes, they stoned Paul and dragged him out of the city, supposing him to be dead. However, when the disciples gathered around him, he rose up and went into the city. And the next day he departed with Barnabas to Derbe" (vv. 19-20). Paul's being "stoned" is noted elsewhere (2 Cor. 11:25a); his being rejected is noted *everywhere*; and his determination to persevere is also constant throughout.

Luke concluded his account of Paul's first trip with an interesting summary. "And when they had preached the gospel to that city and made many disciples, they returned to Lystra, Iconium, and Antioch, strengthening the souls of the disciples, exhorting them to continue in the faith, and saying, 'We must through many tribulations enter the kingdom of God'" (vv. 21-22). Though the notion of experiencing "suffering" seems to have fallen into disrepute in some churches today—they teach that signs of glory, success, and worldly acclaim are the benchmarks by which spirituality is recognized—Paul taught that "followers" must "follow" the Master, and this means difficulties every now and again.

Believing that the movement needed structure, Paul appointed leaders for the communities and left for home:

> 14:23 So when they had appointed elders in every church, and prayed with fasting, they commended them to the Lord in whom they had believed. 24 And after they had passed through Pisidia, they came to Pamphylia. 25 Now when they had preached the word in Perga, they went down to Attalia. 26 From there they sailed to Antioch, where they had been commended to the grace of God for the work which they had completed.

Paul returned to his home base and gave a report: "Now when they had come and gathered the church together, they reported all that God had done with them, and that He had opened the door of faith to the Gentiles. So they stayed there a long time with the disciples." (vv. 27-28). Given the cosmopolitan nature of the church at Antioch, one would expect Paul's message and innovative methods to be well received—and they were.

Just as Paul was a controversial figure before he came to faith, Luke reminds us that Paul was equally controversial afterward. Paul was doing something new: taking the message of Israel's Messiah beyond Israel's borders. He was breaking new ground with his methods, and the message itself was cutting edge: gentiles needn't become Jews to be considered full-fledged members of Israel's commonwealth—they had been "grafted" into a new arrangement. This was a new idea and a few people were understandably confused by this. Innovation, as we know, often prompts confrontation; and this was no exception.

# The *Acts* of the Apostle Paul

## Trip to Jerusalem, ca. 37-38AD    *Acts 15:4-15:29*

Luke relates that "certain men came down from Judea and taught the brethren, 'Unless you are circumcised according to the custom of Moses, you cannot be saved'" (15:1). Paul, of course, would have none of this. "Therefore, when Paul and Barnabas had no small dissension and dispute with them, they determined that Paul and Barnabas and certain others of them should go up to Jerusalem, to the apostles and elders, about this question" (v. 2). "No small dissension" was surely an all-out fight. The need to appeal to the elders of Jerusalem shows that the groundswell of discontent was so great they didn't have the intellectual resources to combat it; so, wanting resolution for the growing tensions, they felt it necessary to appeal to the Apostles in Jerusalem, who, until this point, are missing from Luke's narrative. That they don't appear until now, and then mainly to ratify Paul's ministry, shows their relative unimportance in Luke's narrative. He wants to tell Paul's story and the elders' value is in how they accept the man and endorse the message.

From Luke's account, we can conclude that people were generally pleased by the turn of events. "So, being sent on their way by the church, they passed through Phoenicia and Samaria, describing the conversion of the Gentiles; and they caused great joy to all the brethren" (v. 3)...well, not quite all.

"When they had come to Jerusalem, they were received by the church and the apostles and the elders; and they reported all things that God had done with them. But some of the sect of the Pharisees who believed rose up, saying, 'It is necessary to circumcise them, and to command them to keep the law of Moses'" (vv. 4-5). There was probably more on the table than this point alone, but it underscores the basic nature of the rift—whether non-Jews who wanted to follow Jesus needed to also follow the Mosaic law.

> 15:6 Now the apostles and elders came together to consider this matter. 7 And when there had been much dispute, Peter rose up and said to them: "Men and brethren, you know that a good while ago God chose among us, that by my mouth the Gentiles should hear the word of the gospel and believe. 8 So God, who knows the heart, acknowledged them by giving them the Holy Spirit, just as He did to us, 9 and made no distinction between us and them, purifying their hearts by faith. 10 Now therefore, why do you test God by putting a yoke on the neck of the disciples which neither our fathers nor we were able to bear? 11 But we believe that through the grace of the Lord Jesus Christ we shall be saved in the same manner as they."

Luke is reminding us that the question of including gentiles was previously settled under Peter's administration. The encounter with Cornelius that Peter brings up in 15:7-9 is the story Luke told in Acts 10:1-48 of how a reluctant Peter was directed in a dream to minister to Cornelius, an eager and earnest non-Jew. Peter put his

# The *Acts* of the Apostle Paul

discomfort aside and went to an "unclean" gentile's home (for the very first time!), where he was warmly received and where the Holy Spirit fell upon them.

In both cases (Peter in Acts 10 and Paul in Acts 15), the Jewish Believers were confused about what to do with gentile converts to Jesus. Luke points out the pattern: Jewish Believers are taken aback by the gentiles and contend with Peter/Paul over the matter. The Jewish Believers in Jerusalem had come to terms with gentile inclusion at Peter's urging: "when they heard the things [spoken by Peter]... they became silent; and they glorified God, saying, 'Then God has also granted to the Gentiles repentance to life'" (11:18). Luke's reason for reviewing this point now is simple: the case had already been decided—and in favor of the non-Jews.

Luke continues his story of Paul, briefly mentioning the testimony of Paul and Barnabas in 15:12: "Then all the multitude kept silent and listened to Barnabas and Paul declaring how many miracles and wonders God had worked through them among the Gentiles." Here, as elsewhere, God's personal endorsement of the ministry is offered through evidence of miracles. Luke's recollection of Paul's defense is as follows: Peter did it; and now Paul is following a precedent set by him—with miracles as a further proof. When Jesus' half-brother, James, himself a noteworthy member of the Jerusalem congregation, weighed in on behalf of Paul, the vote was sealed—and in Paul's favor.

> 15:13 And after they had become silent, James answered, saying, "Men and brethren, listen to me: 14 Simon has declared how God at the first visited the Gentiles to take out of them a people for His name. 15 And with this the words of the prophets agree, just as it is written: 16 'After this I will return And will rebuild the tabernacle of David, which has fallen down; I will rebuild its ruins, And I will set it up; 17 so that the rest of mankind may seek the Lord, Even all the Gentiles who are called by My Name, Says the Lord who does all these things.'"

Even though this was an abbreviated account of what happened, the net result was that Paul prevailed. James said:

> 15:19 Therefore I judge that we should not trouble those from among the Gentiles who are turning to God, 20 but that we write to them to abstain from things polluted by idols, from sexual immorality, from things strangled, and from blood. 21 For Moses has had throughout many generations those who preach him in every city, being read in the synagogues every Sabbath

The Messianic Jews in Jerusalem took a welcoming approach by issuing rules that made room for non-Jews who adhered to minimal standards.

Thus concluded, Luke says:

# The *Acts* of the Apostle Paul

15:22 Then it pleased the apostles and elders, with the whole church, to send chosen men of their own company to Antioch with Paul and Barnabas, namely, Judas who was also named Barsabas, and Silas, leading men among the brethren. 23 They wrote this letter by them:

The apostles, the elders, and the brethren,
To the brethren who are of the Gentiles in Antioch, Syria, and Cilicia:

Greetings.

24 Since we have heard that some who went out from us have troubled you with words, unsettling your souls, saying, "You must be circumcised and keep the law"—to whom we gave no such commandment—25 it seemed good to us, being assembled with one accord, to send chosen men to you with our beloved Barnabas and Paul, 26 men who have risked their lives for the name of our Lord Jesus Christ. 27 We have therefore sent Judas and Silas, who will also report the same things by word of mouth. 28 For it seemed good to the Holy Spirit, and to us, to lay upon you no greater burden than these necessary things: 29 that you abstain from things offered to idols, from blood, from things strangled, and from sexual immorality. If you keep yourselves from these, you will do well.

# In the Footsteps of the Rabbi from Tarsus

Farewell.

Again, the so called "Acts of the Apostles" says precious little about the Apostles collectively. What we find interesting are the activities of the Apostle Paul—Luke's companion—and Luke's defense of them. Here, a "Council of the Elders" is convened, but the acts of these Apostles seems confined to their endorsement of Luke's Apostle—Paul.

Vindicated by a ruling that went in their favor, when Paul and his group "were sent off, they came to Antioch; and when they had gathered the multitude together, they delivered the letter." Then, "When they had read it," Luke says that "they rejoiced over its encouragement"— as did he. He closes the narrative noting that "Paul and Barnabas also remained in Antioch, teaching and preaching the word of the Lord, with many others also" (vv. 30-35).

## Paul's Second Journey, 49-52AD    *Acts 15:36-18:22*

Paul's second missionary journey was inspired by an urge to repeat the first one. "Then after some days," says Luke, "Paul said to Barnabas, 'Let us now go back and visit our brethren in every city where we have preached the word of the Lord, and see how they are doing'" (v. 36). The first trip had been successful; and, with new congregations to nurture, Paul was prompted to re-visit them and encourage them in their new-found faith. But that's not what happened, much to Paul's dismay.

# The *Acts* of the Apostle Paul

Paul experienced difficulties right from the start. The Paul-Barnabas team cratered immediately. John Mark—a close relative of Barnabas, who had accompanied Paul and him on the previous journey but then abandoned them—wants to have another shot at it. Barnabas was inclined to take him along, given the family connection. But Paul didn't think it was a good idea. "Now Barnabas was determined to take with them John called Mark. But Paul insisted that they should not take with them the one who had departed from them in Pamphylia, and had not gone with them to the work" (15:37-38). They never were able to come to terms. "Then the contention became so sharp that they parted from one another. And so Barnabas took Mark and sailed to Cyprus; but Paul chose Silas and departed, being commended by the brethren to the grace of God. And he went through Syria and Cilicia, strengthening the churches" (vv. 39-41). As unfortunate as the split was, it seems that good things came of it because now there were two missionary teams out-and-about and not just one.

Whenever Paul suffered the loss of friends and associates, God provided him with others. In 16:1, readers learn that "he came to Derbe and Lystra. And behold, a certain disciple was there, named Timothy, the son of a certain Jewish woman who believed, but his father was Greek." This fellow—with his mother and grandmother—would form endearing friendships with Paul.

In v. 2, Luke informs that Timothy "was well spoken of by the brethren who were at Lystra and Iconium," and that "Paul wanted to have him go on with him." Luke records that Paul took Timothy "and circumcised him because of the Jews who were in that region, for they all knew that his father was Greek" (vv. 2-3) Some think that Paul's wanting to be compliant with Jewish mores is a contradiction, but I don't. Paul did not pretend to be Jewish sometimes and then disparage being Jewish at other times. No—Paul was always a faithful Jew.

In other places and at other times, Paul takes issue with those who mandate that individuals of non-Jewish extract must be circumcised. So, some wonder why, in Timothy's case, he seems to violate his position and encourage Timothy's circumcision. Timothy, however, was a Jew—something we know because of the reference to his Jewish mother. True, his father was a gentile, but Timothy was Jewish nevertheless. Paul's advocating that Timothy comply with Jewish law reveals that Paul did not believe that Jews need to abandon being Jewish in order to follow Israel's Messiah. Instead, Paul maintained that non-Jewish Believers needn't become Jews and adhere to Mosaic law in order to be more acceptable to God. Paul's position, by the way, is a Jewish understanding—one abundantly demonstrated in the Jerusalem Council's verdict noted above.

That said, and the business with Timothy resolved, Paul continued to travel about and inform the churches of the Council's decisions—to good effect. "And as they went through the cities, they delivered to them the decrees to

# The *Acts* of the Apostle Paul

keep, which were determined by the apostles and elders at Jerusalem. So the churches were strengthened in the faith, and increased in number daily" (vv. 4-5). Things seemed to be going well; but then Paul hit a wall—one that he never quite recovered from.

Luke notes in v. 6 that "when they had gone through Phrygia and the region of Galatia, they were forbidden by the Holy Spirit to preach the word in Asia," and that "after they had come to Mysia, they tried to go into Bithynia, but the Spirit did not permit them" (vv. 6-7). Unlike the first trip, it seems that nothing was happening! Paul couldn't open his mouth. It must have been quite frustrating for him; and I'm sure it cost him more than one sleepless night.

The narrative continues: "So passing by Mysia, they came down to Troas" (v. 8), a city situated at one of the westernmost parts of Asia Minor (modern Turkey), "and a vision appeared to Paul in the night. A man of Macedonia stood and pleaded with him, saying, Come over to Macedonia and help us'" (v. 9). Paul immediately sought to go to Macedonia, concluding, Luke says "that the Lord had called us to preach the gospel to them" (v. 10). Had everything gone well in Asia Minor, Paul might have been less motivated to seek the Lord for new opportunities and might even have been less inclined to respond when they were presented. A frustrated Paul was ready to get into something—and get into things he did.

# In the Footsteps of the Rabbi from Tarsus

"Therefore, sailing from Troas, we ran a straight course to Samothrace, and the next day came to Neapolis, and from there to Philippi, which is the foremost city of that part of Macedonia, a colony." The pronoun *we* underscores that Luke had now joined the troop—another sign of Paul's picking up new friends along the way. "And we were staying in that city for some days," continues Luke, when "on the Sabbath day we went out of the city to the riverside, where prayer was customarily made; and we sat down and spoke to the women who met there." The Apostle to the Gentiles made it a habit to visit the Jews wherever he was. He didn't do it to steal Jewish sheep away from being Jewish. He did it because he was a Jew. He living like one and fellowshipped among Jews. In the process, he developed relationships with Jews and was given opportunities to speak in synagogues where he shared Jesus. In this case, "a certain woman named Lydia heard us," reports Luke. "She was a seller of purple," that is a fine clothier and a woman of means, "from the city of Thyatira, who worshiped God. The Lord opened her heart to heed the things spoken by Paul. And when she and her household were baptized, she begged us, saying, 'If you have judged me to be faithful to the Lord, come to my house and stay.' So she persuaded us" (vv. 11-15). One can sense the momentum shifting: though Paul was dead in the water in Asia Minor, it seems that the Lord now opened new doors—providing new opportunities, new friends, and supporters for His servant, Paul.

# The *Acts* of the Apostle Paul

But spiritual enemies were present as well, as shown by the following story (v. 16-18a): "Now it happened, as we went to prayer, that a certain slave girl possessed with a spirit of divination met us, who brought her masters much profit by fortunetelling. This girl followed Paul and us, and cried out, saying, 'These men are the servants of the Most High God, who proclaim to us the way of salvation.' And this she did for many days." Finally Paul had had enough. "But Paul, greatly annoyed, turned and said to the spirit, 'I command you in the name of Jesus Christ to come out of her.' And he came out that very hour. But when her masters saw that their hope of profit was gone, they seized Paul and Silas and dragged them into the marketplace to the authorities. And they brought them to the magistrates, and said, 'These men, being Jews, exceedingly trouble our city; and they teach customs which are not lawful for us, being Romans, to receive or observe'" (vv. 18b-21).

Here we see Paul's ability to overpower demonic forces. Though the supernatural element of Paul's ministry surfaces here, the fact that people hate Paul because of jealousy comes out as well. People who were making profit from this poor girl were upset because her deliverance became a financial liability for them. Unlike Paul, they are shown as having no interest in the girl, whereas Paul is guilty only of helping her. The unreasonableness of Paul's enemies is apparent here and reminds readers of the precariousness of the Gospel enterprise.

# In the Footsteps of the Rabbi from Tarsus

"Then the multitude rose up together against them; and the magistrates tore off their clothes and commanded them to be beaten with rods. And when they had laid many stripes on them, they threw them into prison, commanding the jailer to keep them securely. Having received such a charge," says Luke, "he put them into the inner prison and fastened their feet in the stocks" (vv. 22-24). Busted—and unfairly at that!

So much for the bad news.

"At midnight Paul and Silas were praying and singing hymns to God, and the prisoners were listening to them," and likely wondering how they could be so happy given their circumstances. "Suddenly," says the writer, "there was a great earthquake, so that the foundations of the prison were shaken; and immediately all the doors were opened and everyone's chains were loosed. And the keeper of the prison, awaking from sleep and seeing the prison doors open, supposing the prisoners had fled, drew his sword and was about to kill himself," knowing that he would be blamed and executed for the prisoners' escape. "But Paul called with a loud voice, saying, 'Do yourself no harm, for we are all here.' Then [the guard] called for a light, ran in, and fell down trembling before Paul and Silas. And he brought them out and said, 'Sirs, what must I do to be saved?'" Caught up in the moment and the miracle, the Lord impressed upon (the keeper's] heart that the unique circumstances—and Paul's response to those circumstances—showed that he was in the presence of something that defied reason. Something he

# The *Acts* of the Apostle Paul

attributed to the Divine. "So they said, 'Believe on the Lord Jesus Christ, and you will be saved, you and your household.' Then they spoke the word of the Lord to him and to all who were in his house. And he took them the same hour of the night and washed their stripes. And immediately he and all his family were baptized. Now when he had brought them into his house, he set food before them; and he rejoiced, having believed in God with all his household" (vv. 25-34).

Saying twice that "all his household" came to faith impresses upon readers how the Gospel often flows through family relationships. God's favor, in this case, extended further still: they were released. "And when it was day, the magistrates sent the officers, saying, 'Let those men go.' So the keeper of the prison reported these words to Paul, saying, 'The magistrates have sent to let you go. Now therefore depart, and go in peace'" (vv. 35-36).

But Paul wasn't ready to simply walk out of town. No sir.

In v. 37 Paul responded that the magistrates had openly beaten him and Silas—Roman citizens with no judgments against them—and had thrown them into prison. "And now do they put us out secretly? No indeed! Let them come themselves and get us out.'" Oops. Realizing their criminal actions, the officers told Paul's words to the magistrates, who were afraid when they heard that Paul and Silas were Romans. "Then they came and pleaded with them and brought them out, and asked them to

85

depart from the city" (v. 39). Paul apparently relented. "So they went out of the prison and entered the house of Lydia; and when they had seen the brethren, they encouraged them and departed" (v. 40).

Moving on to chapter 17, Luke says that "when they had passed through Amphipolis and Apollonia, they came to Thessalonica, where there was a synagogue of the Jews. Then Paul, as his custom was, went in to them, and for three Sabbaths reasoned with them from the Scriptures, explaining and demonstrating that the Christ had to suffer and rise again from the dead, and saying, 'This Jesus whom I preach to you is the Christ'" (vv. 1-3). That it was the Rabbi from Tarsus' "custom" to go to synagogues is shown here again, as is the fact that he made his constant appeal to Jesus' Messiahship on the basis of His fulfilling Old Testament predictions. In addition, Luke shows that Paul continued to invoked the ire of others.

> 17:4 And some of them were persuaded and a great multitude of the devout Greeks, and not a few of the leading women, joined Paul and Silas.
>
> 5 But the Jews who were not persuaded, becoming envious, took some of the evil men from the marketplace, and gathering a mob, set all the city in an uproar and attacked the house of Jason, and sought to bring them out to the people. 6 But when they did not find them, they dragged Jason and some brethren to the rulers of the city, crying out, "These who have turned the world upside down

have come here too. 7 Jason has harbored them, and these are all acting contrary to the decrees of Caesar, saying there is another king—Jesus." 8 And they troubled the crowd and the rulers of the city when they heard these things. 9 So when they had taken security from Jason and the rest, they let them go.

It was a sure cause of grief when recent converts to Judaism, along with some prominent women, joined the ranks, and this prompted the mob action. Unable to get their hands on the chief culprits—Paul and company—the unreasonable mob vented their fury on those close to them—the ones who gave Paul's group lodging.

Sensing the imminent danger, "the brethren immediately sent Paul and Silas away by night to Berea." However, Paul and Silas walked right back into danger: "when they arrived, they went into the synagogue of the Jews" (v. 10). Happily, according to the Text, "these were more fair-minded than those in Thessalonica, in that they received the word with all readiness, and searched the Scriptures daily to find out whether these things were so. Therefore many of them believed, and also not a few of the Greeks, prominent women as well as men" (vv. 11-12). "But," as was the case previously and oftentimes thereafter, "when the Jews from Thessalonica learned that the word of God was preached by Paul at Berea, they came there also and stirred up the crowds" (17:13). Again, as before, concerned "brethren sent Paul away, to go to the sea; but both Silas and Timothy remained

# In the Footsteps of the Rabbi from Tarsus

there." Circumstances forced Paul farther south: "So those who conducted Paul brought him to Athens; and receiving a command for Silas and Timothy to come to him with all speed, they departed" (vv. 14-15).

Paul showed himself to be flexible while he was in Athens. Though the Apostle to the Gentiles could always count on a synagogue to visit and get things going, in Athens he made a bigger bid outside the Jewish sphere than inside—and with lackluster results. Anxious to tell the story to non-Jews particularly, he told it openly in Athens. But the Athenians did not have the pre-understanding from the Scriptures that helped his other non-Jewish converts; so, his haravest was rather lean, to put it mildly.

In v.16, Luke reports that "while Paul waited for them [Silas and Timothy] at Athens, his spirit was provoked within him when he saw that the city was given over to idols." "He reasoned in the synagogue with the Jews and with the Gentile worshipers," as was his habit, "and in the marketplace daily with those who happened to be there. Then certain Epicurean and Stoic philosophers encountered him. And some said, 'What does this babbler want to say?' Others said, 'He seems to be a proclaimer of foreign gods,' because he preached to them Jesus and the resurrection" (vv. 17-18). Even here, Paul is represented as a Jewish preacher, advocating for a Jewish concept—the resurrection of the dead—albeit with a Jesus twist.

# The *Acts* of the Apostle Paul

In vv. 19-20, Luke reports that some are a little open: "And they took him and brought him to the Areopagus, saying, 'May we know what this new doctrine is of which you speak? For you are bringing some strange things to our ears. Therefore we want to know what these things mean." Then Luke tells us that "all the Athenians and the foreigners who were there spent their time in nothing else but either to tell or to hear some new thing" (v. 21), a statement that seems to confirm the notion that people were receptive.

Paul continued—or, rather, Luke continues telling Paul's story:

> 17:22 Then Paul stood in the midst of the Areopagus [Court of Athens] and said, "Men of Athens, I perceive that in all things you are very religious; 23 for as I was passing through and considering the objects of your worship, I even found an altar with this inscription:
>
> To The Unknown God.
>
> Therefore, the One whom you worship without knowing, Him I proclaim to you: 24 God, who made the world and everything in it, since He is Lord of heaven and earth, does not dwell in temples made with hands. 25 Nor is He worshiped with men's hands, as though He needed anything, since He gives to all life, breath, and all things.

# In the Footsteps of the Rabbi from Tarsus

26 And He has made from one blood every nation of men to dwell on all the face of the earth, and has determined their pre-appointed times and the boundaries of their dwellings, 27 so that they should seek the Lord, in the hope that they might grope for Him and find Him, though He is not far from each one of us; 28 for in Him we live and move and have our being, as also some of your own poets have said, 'For we are also His offspring.' 29 Therefore, since we are the offspring of God, we ought not to think that the Divine Nature is like gold or silver or stone, something shaped by art and man's devising. 30 Truly, these times of ignorance God overlooked, but now commands all men everywhere to repent, 31 because He has appointed a day on which He will judge the world in righteousness by the Man whom He has ordained. He has given assurance of this to all by raising Him from the dead."

The upshot was that "when they heard of the resurrection of the dead, some mocked, while others said, 'We will hear you again on this matter.' So Paul departed from among them. However, some men joined him and believed, among them Dionysius the Areopagite, a woman named Damaris, and others with them" (vv. 32-34).

Having invested his energies in Athens, the intrepid missionary now pressed onward toward Corinth, where he made new friends, new enemies, and broke new ground for the Kingdom.

# The *Acts* of the Apostle Paul

In 18:1-3, Luke writes that "Paul departed from Athens and went to Corinth. And he found a certain Jew named Aquila, born in Pontus, who had recently come from Italy with his wife Priscilla (because Claudius had commanded all the Jews to depart from Rome); and he came to them"—because they were in the same line of work.

Roman policy toward Jews had been vacillating: some administrations were friendly, some not. In this case, Claudius was not; and he had expelled Jews such as Aquila and Priscilla from the capital city.

On the move himself—though for other reasons—and of the same trade, Paul linked up with the couple: "So, because he was of the same trade, he stayed with them and worked; for by occupation they were tentmakers" (v. 3). They would become lifelong friends—some of Paul's most loyal.

As was Paul's custom, "he reasoned in the synagogue every Sabbath, and persuaded both Jews and Greeks" to follow Israel's Messiah—Yeshua/Jesus (v. 4).

Encouraged "when Silas and Timothy had come from Macedonia, Paul was compelled by the Spirit, and testified to the Jews that Jesus is the Christ" (v. 5). Nothing new here, and v. 6 shows a pattern: "But when they opposed him and blasphemed, he shook his garments and said to them, 'Your blood be upon your own heads; I am clean. From now on I will go to the Gentiles.'" Let me stress again

# In the Footsteps of the Rabbi from Tarsus

that this reflects no shift in Paul'ssentiment toward Jewish people. The Rabbi from Tarsus is simply noting, as we have seen him do previously, that when his ministry in the synagogue had run its course, he would go elsewhere—and create a Messianic synagogue (what we'd call a "church"), one friendly toward his message.

In v. 7, Luke says "he departed from there and entered the house of a certain man named Justus, one who worshiped God, whose house was next door to the synagogue"; and as luck would have it, "Crispus, the ruler of the synagogue"—the one they had just left—"believed on the Lord with all his household. And many of the Corinthians, hearing, believed and were baptized" (v. 8). A good day, to be sure!

Then the Lord gave Paul a big dose of encouragement: "Now the Lord spoke to Paul in the night by a vision, 'Do not be afraid, but speak, and do not keep silent; for I am with you, and no one will attack you to hurt you; for I have many people in this city'" vv. 9-10. Elsewhere, we'll hear Paul voicing that people were always abandoning him—Church people, I might add. Feeling alone from time to time, Paul took consolation in the fact that God never left him. Even so, because dealing with people can take a toll, Paul had his darker moments. It was no doubt a high-water mark for him to receive best friends Aquila and Priscilla, and to receive the head of the Corinthian synagogue into the ranks of Believers in the new congregation—all supporters of Paul.

# The *Acts* of the Apostle Paul

Paul's Corinthian stay was rather lengthy. In v. 11, Luke says that "he continued there a year and six months, teaching the word of God among them." In the course of time, however, the honeymoon ended. The joy he experienced from his successes was marred by a lack of success; for, "when Gallio was proconsul of Achaia, the Jews with one accord rose up against Paul and brought him to the judgment seat, saying, 'This fellow persuades men to worship God contrary to the law'" (vv. 12-13). The ecstasy turned to agony, as the offensive Paul was once more placed on the defensive.

Paul prevailed this time because the authorities rightly understood that the locals were simply jealous and stirring up arguments as a result. Paul not only prevailed at the hearing, but his accusers were reprimanded afterward! Luke notes that "when Paul was about to open his mouth," at the hearing, "Gallio said to the Jews, 'If it were a matter of wrongdoing or wicked crimes, O Jews, there would be reason why I should bear with you. But if it is a question of words and names and your own law, look to it yourselves; for I do not want to be a judge of such matters.' And he drove them from the judgment seat. Then all the Greeks took Sosthenes, the ruler of the synagogue, and beat him before the judgment seat. But Gallio took no notice of these things" (vv. 14-17).

It is significant that Luke draws attention to the fact that the civic administrators rightly perceived that Paul was no scoundrel, and was not violating any laws. Not only does Luke want to demonstrate to his readers that Paul was Torah compliant (that he was a good and observant Jew, albeit a Jew for Jesus), but that he was also a good citizen of Rome.

Driven more by an inner urge than by demanding circumstances, Paul "took leave of the brethren and sailed for Syria, and Priscilla and Aquila were with him" (v. 18). Being Torah-observant, Paul "had his hair cut off at Cenchrea"—on the coast—"for he had taken a vow." This was a custom among Jews. Having taken leave of Achaia (in southern Greece), Luke says in v. 19 that "he came to Ephesus, and left them there; but he himself entered the synagogue and reasoned with the Jews," as was his habit. When the disciples "asked him to stay a longer time with them, he did not consent, but took leave of them, saying, 'I must by all means keep this coming feast in Jerusalem; but I will return again to you, God willing.' And he sailed from Ephesus" (vv. 20-21). Off he went—again.

Paul's desire to "keep the feast" underscores his position *within* Judaism. Returning to his "home church" kept him connected to his spiritual roots. "And when he had landed at Caesarea, and gone up and greeted the church, he went down to Antioch"—his base (v. 22)—thus concluding his second missionary journey.

## Paul's Third Journey, 53-57AD   *Acts 18:23-21:15*
Paul could be counted upon to take a "pit stop" every now and again. But he was so restless that he could also be counted upon to get "the itch" and venture forth

again. In 18:23, Luke tells us, "After he had spent some time there, he departed and went over the region of Galatia and Phrygia in order, strengthening all the disciples." Luke describes Apollos:

> 18:24 Now a certain Jew named Apollos, born at Alexandria, an eloquent man and mighty in the Scriptures, came to Ephesus. 25 This man had been instructed in the way of the Lord; and being fervent in spirit, he spoke and taught accurately the things of the Lord, though he knew only the baptism of John. 26 So he began to speak boldly in the synagogue. When Aquila and Priscilla heard him, they took him aside and explained to him the way of God more accurately. 27 And when he desired to cross to Achaia, the brethren wrote, exhorting the disciples to receive him; and when he arrived, he greatly helped those who had believed through grace; 28 for he vigorously refuted the Jews publicly, showing from the Scriptures that Jesus is the Christ.

Apollos was an intelligent and eloquent man, possessing a keen disposition that drew people toward him. And he wasn't full of himself, as shown by the fact that he was willing to allow Aquila and Priscilla to "pull him aside" and fill in some blanks in his understanding. To be a good teacher one must be teachable and Apollos seems a living model. Having built up equity with the locals, he was commended to the Church at large.

# In the Footsteps of the Rabbi from Tarsus

Having introduced Apollos, Luke says in chapter 19, "it happened, while Apollos was at Corinth, that Paul, having passed through the upper regions, came to Ephesus. And finding some disciples he said to them, 'Did you receive the Holy Spirit when you believed?' So they said to him, 'We have not so much as heard whether there is a Holy Spirit.' And he said to them, 'Into what then were you baptized?' So they said, 'Into John's baptism.'" (vv. 1-3). As was the case with Apollos, people knew of John the Baptist's ministry—Jesus' forerunner—but didn't know of the One to whom he pointed. Paul filled in the gaps.

> 19:4 Then Paul said, "John indeed baptized with a baptism of repentance, saying to the people that they should believe on Him who would come after him, that is, on Christ Jesus."
>
> 5 When they heard this, they were baptized in the name of the Lord Jesus. 6 And when Paul had laid hands on them, the Holy Spirit came upon them, and they spoke with tongues and prophesied. 7 Now the men were about twelve in all.

Luke takes pains to note that Paul's ministry was similar to the ministry of Apollos, whom they admired. Apollos knew only of John's ministry, until updated by Aquila and Priscilla. So too were these Ephesian disciples aware only of John's ministry until Paul helped them to fully understand God's salvation plan.

# The *Acts* of the Apostle Paul

Not only that, in v. 8 we learn that Rabbi Paul—as was his custom—"went into the synagogue and spoke boldly for three months, reasoning and persuading concerning the things of the kingdom of God"; and we learn that, as often happened, "when some were hardened and did not believe, but spoke evil of the Way before the multitude, he departed from them and withdrew the disciples, reasoning daily in the school of Tyrannus. And this continued for two years, so that all who dwelt in Asia heard the word of the Lord Jesus, both Jews and Greeks" (v. 9-10).

Having just noted that "Paul laid hands on them" and that, in response, "the Holy Spirit came upon them," Luke develops the spiritual side of Paul's ministry and gifting. "Now God worked unusual miracles by the hands of Paul," says his biographer, so much so "that even handkerchiefs or aprons were brought from his body to the sick, and the diseases left them and the evil spirits went out of them" (v. 11-12).

Though it's important to note that Paul had these gifts, Luke mentions this to tell us that some outsiders wanted them too. "Then some of the itinerant Jewish exorcists took it upon themselves to call the name of the Lord Jesus over those who had evil spirits, saying, 'We exorcise you by the Jesus whom Paul preaches'" (v. 13). "There were seven sons of Sceva, a Jewish chief priest, who did so. And the evil spirit answered and said, 'Jesus

# In the Footsteps of the Rabbi from Tarsus

I know, and Paul I know; but who are you?'" (vv. 14-15) Try though they might, they could not control the evil forces. In v. 16, Luke says "the man in whom the evil spirit was leaped on them, overpowered them, and prevailed against them, so that they fled out of that house naked and wounded." Spiritual gifts are not something to covet or to play with! These people learned the hard way, did they not?

Now a revival ensued:

> 19:17 This became known both to all Jews and Greeks dwelling in Ephesus; and fear fell on them all, and the name of the Lord Jesus was magnified. 18 And many who had believed came confessing and telling their deeds. 19 Also, many of those who had practiced magic brought their books together and burned them in the sight of all. And they counted up the value of them, and it totaled fifty thousand pieces of silver. 20 So the word of the Lord grew mightily and prevailed.

Signs of revival abounded: they repented, confessed, and told their deeds. They actually turned from their old manner (shown by the torching of their magic books) highlighting the sincerity of their confession. It also explains why those who manufactured idol paraphernalia were upset and would later stage a riot in response to this revival.

Though he was pleased, Paul was inclined to move on. "When these things were accomplished," Luke reminds

# The *Acts* of the Apostle Paul

us, Paul felt impelled by the Holy Spirit to go through Macedonia and Achaia before returning to Jerusalem, saying, "After I have been there, I must also see Rome" (v. 21). Travel-minded and mission-minded, "he sent into Macedonia two of those who ministered to him, Timothy and Erastus, but he himself stayed in Asia for a time" (v. 22). In certain respects, he was alone—and trouble struck in vv. 23-41. I'll provide the entire passage, with my observation to follow.

> 19:23 And about that time there arose a great commotion about the Way. 24 For a certain man named Demetrius, a silversmith, who made silver shrines of Diana, brought no small profit to the craftsmen. 25 He called them together with the workers of similar occupation, and said: "Men, you know that we have our prosperity by this trade. 26 Moreover you see and hear that not only at Ephesus, but throughout almost all Asia, this Paul has persuaded and turned away many people, saying that they are not gods which are made with hands. 27 So not only is this trade of ours in danger of falling into disrepute, but also the temple of the great goddess Diana may be despised and her magnificence destroyed, whom all Asia and the world worship."
>
> 28 Now when they heard this, they were full of wrath and cried out, saying, "Great is Diana of the Ephesians!" 29 So the whole city was filled with confusion, and rushed into the theater with one

**99**

accord, having seized Gaius and Aristarchus, Macedonians, Paul's travel companions. 30 And when Paul wanted to go in to the people, the disciples would not allow him. 31 Then some of the officials of Asia, who were his friends, sent to him pleading that he would not venture into the theater. 32 Some therefore cried one thing and some another, for the assembly was confused, and most of them did not know why they had come together. 33 And they drew Alexander out of the multitude, the Jews putting him forward. And Alexander motioned with his hand, and wanted to make his defense to the people. 34 But when they found out that he was a Jew, all with one voice cried out for about two hours, "Great is Diana of the Ephesians!"

35 And when the city clerk had quieted the crowd, he said: "Men of Ephesus, what man is there who does not know that the city of the Ephesians is temple guardian of the great goddess Diana, and of the image which fell down from Zeus? 36 Therefore, since these things cannot be denied, you ought to be quiet and do nothing rashly. 37 For you have brought these men here who are neither robbers of temples nor blasphemers of your goddess. 38 Therefore, if Demetrius and his fellow craftsmen have a case against anyone, the courts are open and there are proconsuls. Let them bring charges against one another. 39 But if you have any other inquiry to make, it shall be determined in the

# The *Acts* of the Apostle Paul

lawful assembly. 40 For we are in danger of being called in question for today's uproar, there being no reason which we may give to account for this disorderly gathering." 41 And when he had said these things, he dismissed the assembly.

Earlier themes surface here again. Jealous people stirred up the crowd against Paul, who had done nothing wrong and socially-savvy magistrates recognized that Paul was innocent and tried to calm the swelling crowds and restore order. Luke continues in 20:1, noting that Paul left town: "After the uproar had ceased, Paul called the disciples to himself, embraced them, and departed to go to Macedonia."

In vv. 2-6, we see Paul encouraging the brethren and organizing his and the Church's affairs. Luke observes that the tide was turning against the Rabbi from Tarsus.

> 20:2 Now when he had gone over that region and encouraged them with many words, he came to Greece 3 and stayed three months. And when the Jews plotted against him as he was about to sail to Syria, he decided to return through Macedonia. 4 And Sopater of Berea accompanied him to Asia— also Aristarchus and Secundus of the Thessalonians, and Gaius of Derbe, and Timothy, and Tychicus and Trophimus of Asia. 5 These men, going ahead, waited for us at Troas. 6 But we sailed away from Philippi after the Days of Unleavened Bread, and in

five days joined them at Troas, where we stayed seven days.

The plot against Paul would thicken—but not just yet.

> 20:7 Now on the first day of the week, when the disciples came together to break bread, Paul, ready to depart the next day, spoke to them and continued his message until midnight. 8 There were many lamps in the upper room where they were gathered together. 9 And in a window sat a certain young man named Eutychus, who was sinking into a deep sleep. He was overcome by sleep; and as Paul continued speaking, he fell down from the third story and was taken up dead. 10 But Paul went down, fell on him, and embracing him said, "Do not trouble yourselves, for his life is in him." 11 Now when he had come up, had broken bread and eaten, and talked a long while, even till daybreak, he departed. 12 And they brought the young man in alive, and they were not a little comforted [they were greatly comforted].

From this we learn that the disciples met on the "first day of the week." Though some offer this as a reason for a Sunday morning Church gathering as opposed to a Sabbath service, we should note that the "first day" is reckoned by the Jewish calendar—with the day beginning at sundown (i.e., in the evening). From the Text we learn that they had a supper meal and that afterward, Paul began to speak. Paul spoke long, and a sleepy fellow fell out the window from the sill where he was seated. He plummeted to the ground and died. Paul prayed for him, assured the others that he would revive, and went back to speak—until sunrise when he departed. As was and is customary among Jews, Paul was having an after-Sabbath party, during which time he broke bread with the disciples and spoke. Because this was not a Sunday morning service, one should not use it as a proof Text for Sunday morning services—the evidence for which is derived from better sources.

In any case, Luke shares some of Paul's itinerary:

> 20:13 Then we went ahead to the ship and sailed to Assos, there intending to take Paul on board; for so he had given orders, intending himself to go on foot. 14 And when he met us at Assos, we took him on board and came to Mitylene. 15 We sailed from there, and the next day came opposite Chios. The following day we arrived at Samos and stayed at Trogyllium. The next day we came to Miletus. 16 For Paul had decided to sail past Ephesus, so that he would not have to spend time in Asia; for he was hurrying to be at Jerusalem, if possible, on the Day of Pentecost.

Paul wasn't moving about aimlessly: he had a mission and was determined to accomplish his objectives—right now, getting to Jerusalem.

# In the Footsteps of the Rabbi from Tarsus

While making a stopover in Ephesus, Luke records some of what Paul shared with the Ephesian elders (vv. 17-35): "From Miletus he sent to Ephesus and called for the elders of the church. And when they had come to him, he said to them: 'You know, from the first day that I came to Asia, in what manner I always lived among you, serving the Lord with all humility, with many tears and trials which happened to me by the plotting of the Jews." Paul was not *against* the Jews as he was talking *to* Jews. As he spoke, he harked back to the trying times he had experienced in the synagogues—something that followed him his entire career. He was in mid-journey to Jerusalem, and that prompted these reflections, for if it was difficult in the synagogues at the outskirts of the empire, one can only imagine what he expected to find in Jerusalem itself. His audience sensed the impending difficulties, as did he. Paul's speech continues in v. 20: "I kept back nothing that was helpful, but proclaimed it to you, and taught you publicly and from house to house, testifying to Jews, and also to Greeks, repentance toward God and faith toward our Lord Jesus Christ. And see, now I go bound in the spirit to Jerusalem, not knowing the things that will happen to me there, except that the Holy Spirit testifies in every city, saying that chains and tribulations await me."

Because Paul and those listening were all mindful of the danger of the journey, emotions ran high. However, Paul saids that "none of these things move me; nor do I count my life dear to myself, so that I may finish my race with joy, and the ministry which I received from the Lord

# The *Acts* of the Apostle Paul

Jesus, to testify to the gospel of the grace of God." Paul was determined to be steadfast. Having reminded them of his determination, he then exhorted them.

> 20:25 "And indeed, now I know that you all, among whom I have gone preaching the kingdom of God, will see my face no more. 26 Therefore I testify to you this day that I am innocent of the blood of all men. 27 For I have not shunned to declare to you the whole counsel of God. 28 Therefore take heed to yourselves and to all the flock, among which the Holy Spirit has made you overseers, to shepherd the church of God which He purchased with His own blood. 29 For I know this, that after my departure savage wolves will come in among you, not sparing the flock. 30 Also from among yourselves men will rise up, speaking perverse things, to draw away the disciples after themselves. 31 Therefore watch, and remember that for three years I did not cease to warn everyone night and day with tears.

> 32 "So now, brethren, I commend you to God and to the word of His grace, which is able to build you up and give you an inheritance among all those who are sanctified. 33 I have coveted no one's silver or gold or apparel. 34 Yes, you yourselves know that these hands have provided for my necessities, and for those who were with me. 35 I have shown you in every way, by laboring like this, that you must support the weak. And remember

# In the Footsteps of the Rabbi from Tarsus

the words of the Lord Jesus, that He said, 'It is more blessed to give than to receive.'"

After saying these things, "he knelt down and prayed with them all" (v. 36). Luke says that "they all wept freely, and fell on Paul's neck and kissed him, sorrowing most of all for the words which he spoke, that they would see his face no more. And they accompanied him to the ship."

Off he went, with his internal compass pointing toward Jerusalem. Luke now takes up Paul's itinerary in chapter 21, where he leads his readers to Israel—with Paul.

> 21:1 Now it came to pass, that when we had departed from them and set sail, running a straight course we came to Cos, the following day to Rhodes, and from there to Patara. 2 And finding a ship sailing over to Phoenicia, we went aboard and set sail. 3 When we had sighted Cyprus, we passed it on the left, sailed to Syria, and landed at Tyre; for there the ship was to unload her cargo.
>
> 4 And finding disciples, we stayed there seven days. They told Paul through the Spirit not to go up to Jerusalem. 5 When we had come to the end of those days, we departed and went on our way; and they all accompanied us, with wives and children, till we were out of the city. And we knelt down on the shore and prayed. 6 When we had taken our

# The *Acts* of the Apostle Paul

leave of one another, we boarded the ship, and they returned home.

7 And when we had finished our voyage from Tyre, we came to Ptolemais, greeted the brethren, and stayed with them one day.

A warning had been given: "Don't go to Jerusalem; bad things will happen to you there"—but Paul was not to be dissuaded, as is shown by the following story.

21:8 On the next day we who were Paul's companions departed and came to Caesarea, and entered the house of Philip the evangelist, who was one of the seven, and stayed with him. 9 Now this man had four virgin daughters who prophesied. 10 And as we stayed many days, a certain prophet named Agabus came down from Judea. 11 When he had come to us, he took Paul's belt, bound his own hands and feet, and said, "Thus says the Holy Spirit, 'So shall the Jews at Jerusalem bind the man who owns this belt, and deliver him into the hands of the Gentiles.'"

12 Now when we heard these things, both we and those from that place pleaded with him not to go up to Jerusalem. 13 Then Paul answered, "What do you mean by weeping and breaking my heart? For I am ready not only to be bound, but also to die at Jerusalem for the name of the Lord Jesus."

14 So when he would not be persuaded, we ceased, saying, "The will of the Lord be done."
15 And after those days we packed and went up to Jerusalem."

… to face whatever the Lord might have for them there.

## Trip to Jerusalem, ca. 48-49AD *Acts 21:16-26:32*

"Some of the disciples from Caesarea went with us," says Luke, "and brought with them a certain Mnason of Cyprus, an early disciple, with whom we were to lodge" (v. 16). He goes on to report in v. 17. that "when we had come to Jerusalem, the brethren received us gladly," but that on the following day, things began to deteriorate. "Paul went in with us to James, and all the elders were present" (v. 18). Paul greeted them and began to tell "in detail those things which God had done among the Gentiles through his ministry" (v. 19).

Initially, "when they heard it, they glorified the Lord. And they said to him, 'You see, brother, how many myriads of Jews there are who have believed, and they are all zealous for the law; but they have been informed about you," Paul, "that you teach all the Jews who are among the Gentiles to forsake Moses, saying that they ought not to circumcise their children nor to walk according to the customs. What then? The assembly must certainly meet, for they will hear that you have come. Therefore do what we tell you: We have four men who have taken a vow. Take them and be purified with them, and pay their expenses so that they may shave their heads, and that all may know that those things of which they were informed concerning you are nothing, but that you yourself also walk orderly and keep the law. But concerning the Gentiles who believe, we have written and decided that they should observe no such thing, except that they should keep themselves from things offered to idols, from blood, from things strangled, and from sexual immorality'" (vv. 20-25).

The "elders" seemed genuinely pleased to see Paul and thrilled to learn of the Gospel's advances under the Rabbi from Tarsus' ministry. Still, Paul's presence among them created certain problems for them. His reputation had predeced him. Apparently, some misconstrued Paul's position that the *gentiles* needn't adhere to a strict inter- pretation of Judaism as his call for *Jews* to abandon the tradition. This surely wasn't the case, but it was their perception. And, in a world where reality was one's perception of it, the misunderstanding was problematic. In order to improve the situation, the leaders suggested that Paul demonstrate his fidelity to the ancestral Jewish religion—something he was very willing to do. The hope was that people would realize that they had misread Paul. Reasonable though it was, the strategy did not work, as unreasonable people were hell-bent on accusing him and attacking him, regardless of the facts.

In any case, "Paul took the men, and the next day, having been purified with them, entered the temple to announce the expiration of the days of purification, at which time an offering should be made for each one of

# In the Footsteps of the Rabbi from Tarsus

them" (v. 26). Trouble came when "Jews from Asia, seeing him in the temple, stirred up the whole crowd and laid hands on him, crying out, 'Men of Israel, help! This is the man who teaches all men everywhere against the people, the law, and this place; and furthermore he also brought Greeks into the temple and has defiled this holy place.' (For they had previously seen Trophimus the Ephesian with him in the city, whom they supposed that Paul had brought into the temple)" (vv. 27-29).

As had happened previously, "all the city was disturbed; and the people ran together, seized Paul, and dragged him out of the temple; and immediately the doors were shut" (v. 30). In response to the civil disturbance, forces were sent:

> 21:31 Now as they were seeking to kill him, news came to the commander of the garrison that all Jerusalem was in an uproar. 32 He immediately took soldiers and centurions, and ran down to them. And when they saw the commander and the soldiers, they stopped beating Paul. 33 Then the commander came near and took him, and commanded him to be bound with two chains; and he asked who he was and what he had done. 34 And some among the multitude cried one thing and some another."

The commander made haste to get there and break up a brawl. Wanting cooler heads to prevail, he tried to understand why they were venting such fury on one of their own. He was unable to come to terms with the reason for this, however. Luke says that "when he could not ascertain the truth because of the tumult, he commanded him to be taken into the barracks. When he reached the stairs, he [Paul] had to be carried by the soldiers because of the violence of the mob. For the multitude of the people followed after, crying out, 'Away with him!'" (vv. 35-36)

> 21:37 Then as Paul was about to be led into the barracks, he said to the commander, "May I speak to you?" He replied, "Can you speak Greek? 38 Are you not the Egyptian who some time ago stirred up a rebellion and led the four thousand assassins out into the wilderness?" 39 But Paul said, "I am a Jew from Tarsus, in Cilicia, a citizen of no mean city; and I implore you, permit me to speak to the people."

The curious and befuddled commander gave an affirmative response.

Luke continues in v. 40. "So when he had given him permission, Paul stood on the stairs and motioned with his hand to the people. And when there was a great silence, he spoke to them in the Hebrew language." In order to present his views in full, I have provideded the Text without interruption, though my comments on 22:1-21 will follow soon enough.

> 22:1 "Brethren and fathers, hear my defense before you now." 2 And when they heard that he spoke to them in the Hebrew language, they kept all the

more silent. Then he said: 3 "I am indeed a Jew, born in Tarsus of Cilicia, but brought up in this city at the feet of Gamaliel, taught according to the strictness of our fathers' law, and was zealous toward God as you all are today. 4 I persecuted this Way to the death, binding and delivering into prisons both men and women, 5 as also the high priest bears me witness, and all the council of the elders, from whom I also received letters to the brethren, and went to Damascus to bring in chains even those who were there to Jerusalem to be punished.

6 "Now it happened, as I journeyed and came near Damascus at about noon, suddenly a great light from heaven shone around me. 7 And I fell to the ground and heard a voice saying to me, 'Saul, Saul, why are you persecuting Me?' 8 So I answered, 'Who are You, Lord?' And He said to me, 'I am Jesus of Nazareth, whom you are persecuting.'

9 "And those who were with me indeed saw the light and were afraid, but they did not hear the voice of Him who spoke to me. 10 So I said, 'What shall I do, Lord?' And the Lord said to me, 'Arise and go into Damascus, and there you will be told all things which are appointed for you to do.' 11 And since I could not see for the glory of that light, being led by the hand of those who were with me, I came into Damascus.

# The *Acts* of the Apostle Paul

22:12 "Then a certain Ananias, a devout man according to the law, having a good testimony with all the Jews who dwelt there, 13 came to me; and he stood and said to me, 'Brother Saul, receive your sight.' And at that same hour I looked up at him. 14 Then he said, 'The God of our fathers has chosen you that you should know His will, and see the Just One, and hear the voice of His mouth. 15 For you will be His witness to all men of what you have seen and heard. 16 And now why are you waiting? Arise and be baptized, and wash away your sins, calling on the name of the Lord.'

17 "Now it happened, when I returned to Jerusalem and was praying in the temple, that I was in a trance 18 and saw Him saying to me, 'Make haste and get out of Jerusalem quickly, for they will not receive your testimony concerning Me.' 19 So I said, 'Lord, they know that in every synagogue I imprisoned and beat those who believe on You. 20 And when the blood of Your martyr Stephen was shed, I also was standing by consenting to his death, and guarding the clothes of those who were killing him.' 21 Then He said to me, 'Depart, for I will send you far from here to the Gentiles.'"

In his opening salvo, Paul shared his conversion story—one of three accounts of it in Acts—and pointed out how he himself once had judicial authorization to bind members of the group and take them away, much as he was now bound himself. His testimony fell on deaf ears, however. In vv. 22-24, Luke goes on to say that they "listened to him until this word, and then they raised their voices and said, 'Away with such a fellow from the earth, for he is not fit to live!' Then, as they cried out and tore off their clothes and threw dust into the air, the commander ordered him to be brought into the barracks, and said that he should be examined under scourging, so that he might know why they shouted so against him." In the heat of the moment, they were bent on his eradication. Their blood thirst knew no bounds.

"And as they bound him with thongs," Luke informs us that "Paul said to the centurion who stood by, 'Is it lawful for you to scourge a man who is a Roman, and uncondemned?'" (v. 25). Having been made aware of Paul's status as a citizen, and mindful of the rights he had by virtue of that standing, "When the centurion heard that, he went and told the commander, saying, 'Take care what you do, for this man is a Roman.' Then the commander came and said to him, 'Tell me, are you a Roman?' He said, 'Yes.' The commander answered, 'With a large sum I obtained this citizenship.' And Paul said, 'But I was born a citizen.' Then immediately those who were about to examine him withdrew from him; and the commander was also afraid after he found out that he was a Roman, and because he had bound him," without adequate due process. (vv. 26-29)

The citizenship-related technicality ultimately did nothing to save Paul. It did, however, hold back the abuse for a time, pressing the administrator to apply the legal

# The *Acts* of the Apostle Paul

process more deliberately—a privilege that went with citizenship—and it provided an audience of elevated political rank to hear Paul's witness. The trial date was set: "The next day, because he wanted to know for certain why he was accused by the Jews, he released him from his bonds, and commanded the chief priests and all their council to appear, and brought Paul down and set him before them" (v. 30).

As Luke provided Paul's initial speech without interruption, I will do little more than reproduce the speech from chapter 23.

> 23:1 Then Paul, looking earnestly at the council, said, "Men and brethren, I have lived in all good conscience before God until this day." 2 And the high priest Ananias commanded those who stood by him to strike him on the mouth. 3 Then Paul said to him, "God will strike you, you whitewashed wall! For you sit to judge me according to the law, and do you command me to be struck contrary to the law?"
>
> 4 And those who stood by said, "Do you revile God's high priest?" 5 Then Paul said, "I did not know, brethren, that he was the high priest; for it is written, 'You shall not speak evil of a ruler of your people.'" 6 But when Paul perceived that one part were Sadducees and the other Pharisees, he cried out in the council, "Men and brethren, I am a Pharisee, the son of a Pharisee; concerning the

> hope and resurrection of the dead I am being judged!"
>
> 7 And when he had said this, a dissension arose between the Pharisees and the 8 Sadducees; and the assembly was divided. For Sadducees say that there is no resurrection—and no angel or spirit; but the Pharisees confess both. 9 Then there arose a loud outcry. And the scribes of the Pharisees' party arose and protested, saying, "We find no evil in this man; but if a spirit or an angel has spoken to him, let us not fight against God."

It is interesting that Paul played the Pharisees against the Sadducees here, but in my estimation it is also worth noting the respect that Paul showed for the High Priest. His knee-jerk response, even when treated unfairly, supports the idea that Paul lived within Jewish mores— and not outside, as was the dispute here. Luke thus positions the Rabbi from Tarsus as standing within Judaism, and as taking heat because of an internal dispute among Jews.

Then, tensions mounted once again. In v. 10, readers learn that "when there arose a great dissension, the commander, fearing lest Paul might be pulled to pieces by them, commanded the soldiers to go down and take him by force from among them, and bring him into the barracks." Luke tells the readers that due process was interfered with by irrational, frenzied mobs bent on destroying Paul for reasons of their own. Responsible

# The *Acts* of the Apostle Paul

Roman administrators are shown as trying to get a handle on the situation, and that their best efforts were thwarted at every turn.

Luke testifies in v.11 that there was a reason behind the madness—a God-ordained reason, in fact. "But the following night the Lord stood by him and said, 'Be of good cheer, Paul; for as you have testified for Me in Jerusalem, so you must also bear witness at Rome.'"

Meantime, this group of Jews was ready to deny justice and violate civic order.

> 23:12 And when it was day, some of the Jews banded together and bound themselves under an oath, saying that they would neither eat nor drink till they had killed Paul. 13 Now there were more than forty who had formed this conspiracy. 14 They came to the chief priests and elders, and said, "We have bound ourselves under a great oath that we will eat nothing until we have killed Paul. 15 Now you, therefore, together with the council, suggest to the commander that he be brought down to you tomorrow, as though you were going to make further inquiries concerning him; but we are ready to kill him before he comes near."
>
> 16 So when Paul's sister's son heard of their ambush, he went and entered the barracks and told Paul. 17 Then Paul called one of the centurions to him and said, "Take this young man

to the commander, for he has something to tell him." 18 So he took him and brought him to the commander and said, "Paul the prisoner called me to him and asked me to bring this young man to you. He has something to say to you." 19 Then the commander took him by the hand, went aside, and asked privately, "What is it that you have to tell me?" 20 And he said, "The Jews have agreed to ask that you bring Paul down to the council tomorrow, as though they were going to inquire more fully about him. 21 But do not yield to them, for more than forty of them lie in wait for him, men who have bound themselves by an oath that they will neither eat nor drink till they have killed him; and now they are ready, waiting for the promise from you."

Here, as just about everywhere else in the New Testament, we should understand the word "Jews" to be a reference to "Judeans," given that the term *Jew* is an abbreviation of *Juedean.* The Jewish people were not collectively given to accusing or harming Paul. This is shown by the fact that the stealthy decision to ambush him was made by only a few dozen. Though Paul was a controversial figure, it is fair to say that he did not disavow Judaism outright and was not spurned by all Jews.

Back to our story: Having learned of the plot of a few, "the commander let the young man depart, and commanded him, 'Tell no one that you have revealed these things to me'" (v. 22). He then made ready a sizable contingent of soldiers, had Paul spirited away under the cover of darkness, and had a letter written to the governor, Felix.

> 23:23 And he called for two centurions, saying, "Prepare two hundred soldiers, seventy horsemen, and two hundred spearmen to go to Caesarea at the third hour of the night; 24 and provide mounts to set Paul on, and bring him safely to Felix the governor." 25 He wrote a letter in the following manner:
>
> 26 Claudius Lysias,
>
> To the most excellent governor Felix:
>
> Greetings.
>
> 27 This man was seized by the Jews and was about to be killed by them. Coming with the troops I rescued him, having learned that he was a Roman. 28 And when I wanted to know the reason they accused him, I brought him before their council. 29 I found out that he was accused concerning questions of their law, but had nothing charged against him deserving of death or chains. 30 And when it was told me that the Jews lay in wait for the man, I sent him immediately to you, and also commanded his accusers to state before you the charges against him.
>
> Farewell.

# In the Footsteps of the Rabbi from Tarsus

Great pain is taken to show that the Romans were giving Paul as fair a deal as possible, and that the trouble stemmed from a powerful and disgruntled Jewish movement—one that was not representative of the sentiments of all the Jews.

In vv. 31-35 we learn that "as they were commanded, [the soldiers] took Paul and brought him by night to Antipatris. The next day they left the horsemen to go on with him, and returned to the barracks. When they came to Caesarea and had delivered the letter to the governor, they also presented Paul to him. And when the governor had read it, he asked what province he was from. And when he understood that he was from Cilicia, he said, 'I will hear you when your accusers also have come.' And he commanded him to be kept in Herod's Praetorium"— a stay that went on for a protracted period of time.

In chapter 24, Luke gives an outline of the charges raised against Paul:

> 24:1 Now after five days Ananias the high priest came down with the elders and a certain orator named Tertullus. These gave evidence to the governor against Paul.
>
> 2 And when he was called upon, Tertullus began his accusation, saying: "Seeing that through you we enjoy great peace, and prosperity is being brought to this nation by your foresight, we accept it always and in all places, most noble Felix, with all

thankfulness. 4 Nevertheless, not to be tedious to you any further, I beg you to hear, by your courtesy, a few words from us. 5 For we have found this man a plague, a creator of dissension among all the Jews throughout the world, and a ringleader of the sect of the Nazarenes. 6 He even tried to profane the temple, and we seized him, and wanted to judge him according to our law. 7 But the commander Lysias came by and with great violence took him out of our hands, 8 commanding his accusers to come to you. By examining him yourself you may ascertain all these things of which we accuse him." 9 And the Jews also assented, maintaining that these things were so.

Paul was called a "plague," a "creator of dissension among Jews," and a "ringleader of the sect of the Nazarenes." The accusation that Paul attempted to "profane the temple" was mentioned while the orator took issue with the Romans having taken Paul from the religious leaders using excessive "violence." Witnesses attested to these things.

It was now Paul's turn.

24:10 Then Paul, after the governor had nodded to him to speak, answered: "Inasmuch as I know that you have been for many years a judge of this nation, I do the more cheerfully answer for myself, 11 because you may ascertain that it is no more than twelve days since I went up to Jerusalem to worship. 12 And they neither found me in the temple disputing with anyone nor inciting the crowd, either in the synagogues or in the city. 13 Nor can they prove the things of which they now accuse me. 14 But this I confess to you, that according to the Way which they call a sect, so I worship the God of my fathers, believing all things which are written in the Law and in the Prophets. 15 I have hope in God, which they themselves also accept, that there will be a resurrection of the dead, both of the just and the unjust. 16 This being so, I myself always strive to have a conscience without offense toward God and men.

17 'Now after many years I came to bring alms and offerings to my nation, 18 in the midst of which some Jews from Asia found me purified in the temple, neither with a mob nor with tumult. 19 They ought to have been here before you to object if they had anything against me. 20 Or else let those who are here themselves say if they found any wrongdoing in me while I stood before the council, 21 unless it is for this one statement which I cried out, standing among them, 'Concerning the resurrection of the dead I am being judged by you this day.'"

Paul seems to have been more respectful in his defense than the prosecution was when presenting their case. Instead of complaining about a Roman intrusion into Jewish affairs—as the prosecution did when drawing attention to Paul's having been wrested free from the mob—Paul expressed measured relief that Felix, an experienced judge, was hearing the case. He noted that his crime was religious in nature and thus really beyond the purview of a Roman court. Paul was arguably playing into a preconceived notion held by the Romans—and one that was not without merit—that some of the Judeans were antagonistic when it came to religious matters, and were at times unreasonable and barely manageable.

When the opening salvos had been fired, Felix chose to put the trial on hold for a time. Luke says that "when Felix heard these things, having more accurate knowledge of the Way, he adjourned the proceedings and said, 'When Lysias the commander comes down, I will make a decision on your case.' So he commanded the centurion to keep Paul and to let him have liberty, and told him not to forbid any of his friends to provide for or visit him" (vv. 22-23). Here also, Romans are represented as being as considerate as possible, given the circumstances. Despite this, Luke notes a problem— one that seems to arise every now and again: judicial corruption.

The story continues:

> 24:24 And after some days, when Felix came with his wife Drusilla, who was Jewish, he sent for Paul and heard him concerning the faith in Christ. 25 Now as he reasoned about righteousness, self-

control, and the judgment to come, Felix was afraid and answered, "Go away for now; when I have a convenient time I will call for you." 26 Meanwhile he also hoped that money would be given him by Paul, that he might release him. Therefore he sent for him more often and conversed with him.

27 But after two years Porcius Festus succeeded Felix; and Felix, wanting to do the Jews a favor, left Paul bound."

Paul didn't give him a dime.

The hearing began again. Luke gives details in chapter 25.

25:1 Now when Festus had come to the province, after three days he went up from Caesarea to Jerusalem. 2 Then the high priest and the chief men of the Jews informed him against Paul; and they petitioned him, 3 asking a favor against him, that he would summon him to Jerusalem—while they lay in ambush along the road to kill him. 4 But Festus answered that Paul should be kept at Caesarea, and that he himself was going there shortly. 5 "Therefore," he said, "let those who have authority among you go down with me and accuse this man, to see if there is any fault in him."

6 And when he had remained among them more than ten days, he went down to Caesarea. And the next day, sitting on the judgment seat, he commanded

# The *Acts* of the Apostle Paul

Paul to be brought. 7 When he had come, the Jews who had come down from Jerusalem stood about and laid many serious complaints against Paul, which they could not prove, 8 while he answered for himself, "Neither against the law of the Jews, nor against the temple, nor against Caesar have I offended in anything at all."

9 But Festus, wanting to do the Jews a favor, answered Paul and said, "Are you willing to go up to Jerusalem and there be judged before me concerning these things?" 10 So Paul said, "I stand at Caesar's judgment seat, where I ought to be judged. To the Jews I have done no wrong, as you very well know. 11 For if I am an offender, or have committed anything deserving of death, I do not object to dying; but if there is nothing in these things of which these men accuse me, no one can deliver me to them. I appeal to Caesar."

12 Then Festus, when he had conferred with the council, answered, "You have appealed to Caesar? To Caesar you shall go!"

Paul couldn't be guaranteed a fair and impartial hearing from the Judean authorities. But his "appeal to Caesar" wasn't made solely on the basis of expecting a fair hearing in Rome, as Luke has noted that corruption was already a factor in the legal proceedings. Paul had been warned more than once that evils awaited him—but he feared not, for Jesus had appeared to him in a dream saying,

# In the Footsteps of the Rabbi from Tarsus

"Be of good cheer, Paul; for as you have testified for Me in Jerusalem, so you must also bear witness at Rome" (23:11). The judicial process was to drag on for some time, but Paul was unconcerned because he knew that he was doing what the Lord wanted him to do. Paul waited patiently, pursuing his calling, and eventually got his day in court. But not before interacting with some interesting characters in Israel.

Luke goes on saying that "after some days King Agrippa and Bernice came to Caesarea to greet Festus."

> 25:14 When they had been there many days, Festus laid Paul's case before the king, saying: "There is a certain man left a prisoner by Felix, 15 about whom the chief priests and the elders of the Jews informed me, when I was in Jerusalem, asking for a judgment against him. 16 To them I answered, 'It is not the custom of the Romans to deliver any man to destruction before the accused meets the accusers face to face, and has opportunity to answer for himself concerning the charge against him.' 17 Therefore when they had come together, without any delay, the next day I sat on the judgment seat and commanded the man to be brought in. 18 When the accusers stood up, they brought no accusation against him of such things as I supposed, 19 but had some questions against him about their own religion and about a certain Jesus, who had died, whom Paul affirmed to be alive. 20 And

# The *Acts* of the Apostle Paul

because I was uncertain of such questions, I asked whether he was willing to go to Jerusalem and there be judged concerning these matters. 21 But when Paul appealed to be reserved for the decision of Augustus, I commanded him to be kept till I could send him to Caesar."

22 Then Agrippa said to Festus, "I also would like to hear the man myself." "Tomorrow," he said, "you shall hear him."

23 So the next day, when Agrippa and Bernice had come with great pomp, and had entered the auditorium with the commanders and the prominent men of the city, at Festus' command Paul was brought in. 24 And Festus said: "King Agrippa and all the men who are here present with us, you see this man about whom the whole assembly of the Jews petitioned me, both at Jerusalem and here, crying out that he was not fit to live any longer. 25 But when I found that he had committed nothing deserving of death, and that he himself had appealed to Augustus, I decided to send him. 26 I have nothing certain to write to my lord concerning him. Therefore I have brought him out before you, and especially before you, King Agrippa, so that after the examination has taken place I may have something to write. 27 For it seems to me unreasonable to send a prisoner and not to specify the charges against him."

# In the Footsteps of the Rabbi from Tarsus

With preliminaries and charges laid out, Luke continues in chapter 26, noting Paul's response.

> 26:1 Then Agrippa said to Paul, "You are permitted to speak for yourself." So Paul stretched out his hand and answered for himself: 2 "I think myself happy, King Agrippa, because today I shall answer for myself before you concerning all the things of which I am accused by the Jews, 3 especially because you are expert in all customs and questions which have to do with the Jews. Therefore I beg you to hear me patiently.
>
> 4 "My manner of life from my youth, which was spent from the beginning among my own nation at Jerusalem, all the Jews know. 5 They knew me from the first, if they were willing to testify, that according to the strictest sect of our religion I lived a Pharisee. 6 And now I stand and am judged for the hope of the promise made by God to our fathers. 7 To this promise our twelve tribes, earnestly serving God night and day, hope to attain. For this hope's sake, King Agrippa, I am accused by the Jews. 8 Why should it be thought incredible by you that God raises the dead?
>
> 9 "Indeed, I myself thought I must do many things contrary to the name of Jesus of Nazareth. 10 This I also did in Jerusalem, and many of the saints I shut up in prison, having received authority from the chief priests; and when they were put to death, I

cast my vote against them. 11 And I punished them often in every synagogue and compelled them to blaspheme; and being exceedingly enraged against them, I persecuted them even to foreign cities.

12 "While thus occupied, as I journeyed to Damascus with authority and commission from the chief priests, 13 at midday, O king, along the road I saw a light from heaven, brighter than the sun, shining around me and those who journeyed with me. 14 And when we all had fallen to the ground, I heard a voice speaking to me and saying in the Hebrew language, 'Saul, Saul, why are you persecuting Me? It is hard for you to kick against the goads.' 15 So I said, 'Who are You, Lord?' And He said, 'I am Jesus, whom you are persecuting. 16 But rise and stand on your feet; for I have appeared to you for this purpose, to make you a minister and a witness both of the things which you have seen and of the things which I will yet reveal to you. 17 I will deliver you from the Jewish people, as well as from the Gentiles, to whom I now send you, 18 to open their eyes, in order to turn them from darkness to light, and from the power of Satan to God, that they may receive forgiveness of sins and an inheritance among those who are sanctified by faith in Me.'

19 "Therefore, King Agrippa, I was not disobedient to the heavenly vision, 20 but declared first to those in Damascus and in Jerusalem, and throughout all

the region of Judea, and then to the Gentiles, that they should repent, turn to God, and do works befitting repentance. 21 For these reasons the Jews seized me in the temple and tried to kill me. 22 Therefore, having obtained help from God, to this day I stand, witnessing both to small and great, saying no other things than those which the prophets and Moses said would come—23 that the Christ would suffer, that He would be the first to rise from the dead, and would proclaim light to the Jewish people and to the Gentiles."

Paul responded to the charges by testifying to his experience and calling. Paul emphasized that he was a religious leader and that he stood before King Agrippa in response to charges that were religious in nature. Convincing as Paul was, Luke says in v. 24, as Paul "made his defense, Festus said with a loud voice, 'Paul, you are beside yourself! Much learning is driving you mad!'"

26:25 But he said, "I am not mad, most noble Festus, but speak the words of truth and reason. 26 For the king, before whom I also speak freely, knows these things; for I am convinced that none of these things escapes his attention, since this thing was not done in a corner. 27 King Agrippa, do you believe the prophets? I know that you do believe."

28 Then Agrippa said to Paul, "You almost persuade me to become a Christian." 29 And Paul

said, "I would to God that not only you, but also all who hear me today, might become both almost and altogether such as I am, except for these chains."

30 When he had said these things, the king stood up, as well as the governor and Bernice and those who sat with them; 31 and when they had gone aside, they talked among themselves, saying, "This man is doing nothing deserving of death or chains." 32 Then Agrippa said to Festus, "This man might have been set free if he had not appealed to Caesar."

From this point on, it was really only a matter of time until the Rabbi from Tarsus got his day in court, in Rome.

## Paul's Fourth Journey, 59-62AD    *Acts 27:1-28:31*

In chapter 27, Luke serves up Paul's itinerary. In 27:1-3, we learn that when it was decided that Paul should sail to Italy, "they delivered Paul and some other prisoners to one named Julius, a centurion of the Augustan Regiment." Luke goes on to say in v. 2 that after they entered "a ship of Adramyttium, we put to sea, meaning to sail along the coasts of Asia. Aristarchus, a Macedonian of Thessalonica, was with us. And the next day we landed at Sidon. And Julius treated Paul kindly and gave him liberty to go to his friends and receive care." So far, so good. "When we had put to sea from there, we sailed under the shelter of Cyprus, because the winds were contrary. And when we had sailed over the sea which is off Cilicia and Pamphylia, we came to Myra, a city of Lycia. There the centurion found an Alexandrian ship sailing to Italy, and he put us on board. When we had sailed slowly many days, and arrived with difficulty off Cnidus, the wind not permitting us to proceed, we sailed under the shelter of Crete off Salmone. Passing it with difficulty, we came to a place called Fair Havens, near the city of Lasea." (vv. 4-8). The "difficulty" referred to in v. 8 was but a portent of things to come.

Whether on land or sea, it seems that Paul's life was always hanging in the balance. The miracle-working, supernaturally-gifted Paul now predicted that trouble was on the horizon. His word was unheeded, however, and the results were disastrous—though not fatal, as we learn from the following lengthy passage.

> 27:9 Now when much time had been spent, and sailing was now dangerous because the Fast was already over, Paul advised them, 10 saying, "Men, I perceive that this voyage will end with disaster and much loss, not only of the cargo and ship, but also our lives." 11 Nevertheless the centurion was more persuaded by the helmsman and the owner of the ship than by the things spoken by Paul. 12 And because the harbor was not suitable to winter in, the majority advised to set sail from there also, if by any means they could reach Phoenix, a harbor of Crete opening toward the southwest and northwest, and winter there.

# The *Acts* of the Apostle Paul

13 When the south wind blew softly, supposing that they had obtained their desire, putting out to sea, they sailed close by Crete. 14 But not long after, a tempestuous head wind arose, called Euroclydon. 15 So when the ship was caught, and could not head into the wind, we let her drive. 16 And running under the shelter of an island called Clauda, we secured the skiff with difficulty. 17 When they had taken it on board, they used cables to undergird the ship; and fearing lest they should run aground on the Syrtis Sands, they struck sail and so were driven. 18 And because we were exceedingly tempest-tossed, the next day they lightened the ship. 19 On the third day we threw the ship's tackle overboard with our own hands. 20 Now when neither sun nor stars appeared for many days, and no small tempest beat on us, all hope that we would be saved was finally given up.

21 But after long abstinence from food, then Paul stood in the midst of them and said, "Men, you should have listened to me, and not have sailed from Crete and incurred this disaster and loss. 22 And now I urge you to take heart, for there will be no loss of life among you, but only of the ship. 23 For there stood by me this night an angel of the God to whom I belong and whom I serve, 24 saying, 'Do not be afraid, Paul; you must be brought before Caesar; and indeed God has granted you all those who sail with you.'

27:25 Therefore take heart, men, for I believe God that it will be just as it was told me. 26 However, we must run aground on a certain island."

27 Now when the fourteenth night had come, as we were driven up and down in the Adriatic Sea, about midnight the sailors sensed that they were drawing near some land. 28 And they took soundings and found it to be twenty fathoms; and when they had gone a little farther, they took soundings again and found it to be fifteen fathoms. 29 Then, fearing lest we should run aground on the rocks, they dropped four anchors from the stern, and prayed for day to come. 30 And as the sailors were seeking to escape from the ship, when they had let down the skiff into the sea, under pretense of putting out anchors from the prow, 31 Paul said to the centurion and the soldiers, "Unless these men stay in the ship, you cannot be saved." 32 Then the soldiers cut away the ropes of the skiff and let it fall off.

33 And as day was about to dawn, Paul implored them all to take food, saying, "Today is the fourteenth day you have waited and continued without food, and eaten nothing. 34 Therefore I urge you to take nourishment, for this is for your survival, since not a hair will fall from the head of any of you." 35 And when he had said these things, he took bread and gave thanks to God in the presence of them all; and when he had broken it

he began to eat. 36 Then they were all encouraged, and also took food themselves. 37 And in all we were two hundred and seventy-six persons on the ship. 38 So when they had eaten enough, they lightened the ship and threw out the wheat into the sea.

39 When it was day, they did not recognize the land; but they observed a bay with a beach, onto which they planned to run the ship if possible. 40 And they let go the anchors and left them in the sea, meanwhile loosing the rudder ropes; and they hoisted the mainsail to the wind and made for shore. 41 But striking a place where two seas met, they ran the ship aground; and the prow stuck fast and remained immovable, but the stern was being broken up by the violence of the waves.

42 And the soldiers' plan was to kill the prisoners, lest any of them should swim away and escape. 43 But the centurion, wanting to save Paul, kept them from their purpose, and commanded that those who could swim should jump overboard first and get to land, 44 and the rest, some on boards and some on parts of the ship. And so it was that they all escaped safely to land.

Luke continues in chapter 28:

28:1 Now when they had escaped, they then found out that the island was called Malta. 2 And the natives showed us unusual kindness; for they kindled a fire and made us all welcome, because of the rain that was falling and because of the cold. 3 But when Paul had gathered a bundle of sticks and laid them on the fire, a viper came out because of the heat, and fastened on his hand. 4 So when the natives saw the creature hanging from his hand, they said to one another, "No doubt this man is a murderer, whom, though he has escaped the sea, yet justice does not allow to live."

5 But he shook off the creature into the fire and suffered no harm. 6 However, they were expecting that he would swell up or suddenly fall down dead. But after they had looked for a long time and saw no harm come to him, they changed their minds and said that he was a god.

7 In that region there was an estate of the leading citizen of the island, whose name was Publius, who received us and entertained us courteously for three days. 8 And it happened that the father of Publius lay sick of a fever and dysentery. Paul went in to him and prayed, and he laid his hands on him and healed him. 9 So when this was done, the rest of those on the island who had diseases also came and were healed. 10 They also honored us in many ways; and when we departed, they provided such things as were necessary.

# The *Acts* of the Apostle Paul

These troubles pretty much behind them, off again they went until they finally arrived in Rome where Paul was placed under something of a "house arrest."

> 28:11 After three months we sailed in an Alexandrian ship whose figurehead was the Twin Brothers, which had wintered at the island. 12 And landing at Syracuse, we stayed three days. 13 From there we circled round and reached Rhegium. And after one day the south wind blew; and the next day we came to Puteoli, 14 where we found brethren, and were invited to stay with them seven days. And so we went toward Rome. 15 And from there, when the brethren heard about us, they came to meet us as far as Appii Forum and Three Inns. When Paul saw them, he thanked God and took courage.
>
> 16 Now when we came to Rome, the centurion delivered the prisoners to the captain of the guard; but Paul was permitted to dwell by himself with the soldier who guarded him.

Paul was innocent and the magistrates in Israel knew it. After telling us that the custodian who was responsible for Paul was kindly disposed toward him, Luke wraps up the acts of the Rabbi from Tarsus with a very interesting story. As Paul was held in Rome, Luke says that Paul requested an audience with the city's Jewish leaders. The meeting was arranged and Paul told his story to them.

# In the Footsteps of the Rabbi from Tarsus

28:17 And it came to pass after three days that Paul called the leaders of the Jews together. So when they had come together, he said to them: "Men and brethren, though I have done nothing against our people or the customs of our fathers, yet I was delivered as a prisoner from Jerusalem into the hands of the Romans, 18 who, when they had examined me, wanted to let me go, because there was no cause for putting me to death. 19 But when the Jews spoke against it, I was compelled to appeal to Caesar, not that I had anything of which to accuse my nation. 20 For this reason therefore I have called for you, to see you and speak with you, because for the hope of Israel I am bound with this chain."

21 Then they said to him, "We neither received letters from Judea concerning you, nor have any of the brethren who came reported or spoken any evil of you. 22 But we desire to hear from you what you think; for concerning this sect, we know that it is spoken against everywhere."

23 So when they had appointed him a day, many came to him at his lodging, to whom he explained and solemnly testified of the kingdom of God, persuading them concerning Jesus from both the Law of Moses and the Prophets, from morning till evening. 24 And some were persuaded by the things which were spoken, and some disbelieved.

# The *Acts* of the Apostle Paul

Luke goes out of his way to present the Jewish leaders in Rome as being a rather fair-minded lot. Since Paul was Jewish and his audience consisted of Jewish leaders, when Paul said that "the Jews spoke against it" in his discourse with them, it should be understood that he was referring to the Judeans—Israelites who resided in the Roman colony—and not the Jews generally. When speaking to the Jewish leaders in Rome, Paul went out of his way to emphasize that he had "done nothing against our people or the customs of our fathers." Assuming this to be correct—and why wouldn't we?—readers are forced to re-evaluate the Rabbi from Tarsus. Though typically represented as having abandoned Judaism and requiring that others abandon it to be "good Christians," it would seem, on the basis of this and related passages, either that Paul is being deceitful here, or that some would do well to re-evaluate their assessment of the man and his message.

Paul's claim, according to Luke, was that he never disparaged the "Law." To the contrary, Luke presents Paul as being Torah-compliant. Nor did Paul ever advocate that the Jews needed to abandon Moses. His point was that gentiles needn't embrace Moses in order to be considered full-fledged members of the Church. This theological nuance might not seem like much at first, but it forces a drastic and much-needed re-evaluation of standard Pauline theology. Today, as yesterday, the misunderstanding is a source of considerable grief.

# In the Footsteps of the Rabbi from Tarsus

These considerations aside, we return now to the narrative itself. Here, in the interest of demonstrating that Paul wasn't universally rejected by the Jewish leaders and that he didn't reject them either, Luke reminds that there was a division among them:

> 28:25 So when they did not agree among themselves, they departed after Paul had said one word: "The Holy Spirit spoke rightly through Isaiah the prophet to our fathers, 26 saying,
>
> 'Go to this people and say: "Hearing you will hear, and shall not understand; And seeing you will see, and not perceive; 27 For the hearts of this people have grown dull. Their ears are hard of hearing, And their eyes they have closed, Lest they should see with their eyes and hear with their ears, Lest they should understand with their hearts and turn, So that I should heal them."'
>
> 28 "Therefore let it be known to you that the salvation of God has been sent to the Gentiles, and they will hear it!" 29 And when he had said these words, the Jews departed and had a great dispute among themselves.
>
> 30 Then Paul dwelt two whole years in his own rented house, and received all who came to him, 31 preaching the kingdom of God and teaching the things which concern the Lord Jesus Christ with all confidence, no one forbidding him.

# The *Acts* of the Apostle Paul

Luke's narrative ends here rather abruptly, with the rabbi still under house arrest. There's a convincing argument that he was released from confinement and that he traveled about for some time afterward. I will save this consideration for the next chapter and bring this chapter to a close noting that the Jewish authorities in Rome were divided among themselves over Paul, as seems to have always been the case.

In bringing Paul's story to a close, Luke reminds us that, as Jews never categorically rejected Jesus (shown by the fact that His first followers were women and men of Jewish extract), the Rabbi from Tarsus was not categorically rejected either. Known as the "Apostle to the Gentiles," Rabbi Paul is represented as forever reaching out to Jewish people. Like Jesus, Paul is not shown as being rejected by everyone. Instead, the community's response was divided—some for Him and him, and others not.

# III

## The *Facts* of the Apostle Paul

### Introduction

The New Testament books of Romans, First and Second Corinthians, Galatians, Ephesians, Philippians, Colossians, First and Second Thessalonians, First and Second Timothy, Titus, and Philemon form the body of Paul's correspondence with the early Church. Beginning in the order of their dating—and *not* the order in which they appear in our New Testaments—we will make *overviews*, *interpretations,* and, most importantly, personal *applications.* This process should bring Bible students to a better comprehension of Paul's ancient writings and help them make responsible, contemporary applications to their own lives and circumstances.

God's written Word is far superior to my own reflections on His Words. For this reason and because this book's purpose is to enhance readers' understanding of Paul and the biblical record's message and meaning, I want to encourage readers to *read the respective Pauline writings first* and then—and only then—proceed to read my reflections on those writings. So, before you read this book's subsection on Galatians, pick up your New Testament and read what Paul wrote there. After reading Paul, come back to this book and read my reflections on his writing. At the end of *my* thoughts, you will find a section in the book to record your own. Following this pattern for each subsection enhances the value of this book, given that its primary purpose is to illuminate Paul's sacred writings, and not to replace them as an authoritative voice for building up good faith and practice. You may or may not agree with my conclusions, but answering the questions at the end of each subsection yourself will help you to crystallize your own understanding of the essence of Pauline faith and practice and also make personal applications. This is principally important; for, at day's end, you are more apt to retain what you teach yourself than whatever I may hope to teach you.

## 1. Paul's Letter to the Church at Galatia
To maximize your spiritual growth and maturation, read *Galatians* now—first. After doing so, feel free to attend to the overview, interpretations, and applications below.

### Introductory Overview
Paul wrote his letter to the Galatians in approximately 49AD, well after Jesus' death and sometime after Paul's first "road trip"—what Bible scholars call his "first missionary journey."

This letter, as all his epistles, reveals that Paul understood and applied the conventions of formal letter writing. For instance, only after giving his standard salutation and introduction did he progress to the letter's body, and then finish with a formal conclusion. Introduction, body, conclusion… It's all quite formal, as you shall see.

As for the body of the Galatians text, the Apostle went on record *boldly taking issue* with religious legalists who postulated that a successful Christian walk for gentiles hinged upon strict adherence to the religious requirements borrowed from Judaism (1:1-10). Paul, on the other hand, didn't believe that following rules would enhance one's spiritual life. The battle lines were drawn and the fight was on.

Paul was *assertive* when he argued his belief that following Jesus brought true freedom. In fact, he was vociferous in *forcefully contending* for the freeing essence

**145**

of authentic Messianic faith and practice. Though he personally appreciated much that was found in the Judaism of the day, Paul didn't agree with those who argued that his followers needed to abide by all of Judaism's sages' interpretations and practices. Paul believed that faith in the Messiah alone would be sufficient for gentiles to be fully pleasing to God.

Using the positions laid out above as his introduction, Paul went on to delineate the essence of "his" grace-full Gospel (2:15-21).

Paul was *not* one of the original Judean disciples; he therefore lacked the firsthand, real-world experience with Jesus that the other Jewish, Galilean-based Apostles had. This prompted some early Jesus Believers to take issue with his innovations and to argue that he really didn't know what he was talking about.

Jesus was a Torah-observant Jew, as were the other Apostles. Paul was an innovator by advocating that being Torah-observant was not an essential ingredient for gentile converts, and his position on this issue caused a quite a stir, as we saw in Acts.

In his letter to the Galatians, *Paul underscored the personal and direct revelation* of his message (1:11-12). That this former anti-Christian's Gospel was uniquely a revelation of his—one not *from* him but given *to* him—and not a message directly passed down through the

# Paul's Letter to the Church at Galatia

early apostolic tradition, he noted in vv. 14-24. Its being "his" and not "theirs" was not much of an issue for Paul; for in Galatians 2:1-10 he noted that the original *Apostles accepted his ministry and message and even endorsed both.* Against that backdrop and given the Apostles' prior endorsement, Paul was perplexed over Peter's vacillation (vv. 11-21)—a problem that plagued the inconsistent Peter through the better part of his life and ministry.

A tendency to create and impose religious traditions surfaced early in the Messianic communities, evidenced by Paul's tackling issues related to it in his earliest writings. It seems a problem today, as well.

Paul's theology of grace took shape as he argued against the rules imposed by Church leaders. In 3:5, Paul stressed *faith in Jesus, over and against rules—even good ones!*—citing Abraham's performance (vv. 6-18). Paul believed that if Abraham—who lived many centuries before Moses—could be righteous before God *without* following the law handed down to Moses, so too could gentiles who had faith in God through Jesus Christ be counted righteous *without* following the Mosaic laws given to Israel. It was a simple and profound argument— and happily, it prevailed.

The "Torah" presaged Jesus' ministry and predicted it accurately, Paul said in 3:19-4:7. He buttressed his point with an allegorical message (4:8-5:12).

# In the Footsteps of the Rabbi from Tarsus

Though Paul did not think gentile Believers needed to submit to Jewish religious legislation, *he clearly did not want them to live without structure.* As we would expect, he spoke about the *Spirit's leading* and the wonderful living and responsibilities that go along with it (5:16-24), contrary to the *flesh*—of which more will be said later. In 5:22-6:5 Paul emphasized *love* and then wrote an exhortation toward *liberality* in 6:6-10—both of which would require moral effort on the part of his followers.

Though Paul was not minded to impose religious Jewish practices on early Believers, he nevertheless required religious practices—moral ones, particularly. Paul instructed his followers to "walk in the Spirit;" thus, they would adhere to the Torah's requirements for moral holiness. He did this without demanding that they follow Jewish dictates word for word. This position agreed with what Jews understood about the responsibility of non-Jews; for Judaism never required that gentiles adhere to the Jewish code as a precondition for gentiles' acceptance by God.

Fearing that Paul was denigrating the sacred and inspired "Law of Moses," however, some of the ill-informed Messianic Jewish followers of Jesus thought Paul was a traitor—a heretic.

In defense, it must be stressed that Paul was *not* advocating that Jews abandon Moses, only that gentiles needn't embrace the contract that God made with the Jewish people. Paul was—and is—misunderstood!

# Paul's Letter to the Church at Galatia

In his day and time, Paul's message was new—and generated disagreement and misunderstanding in the way that "cutting edge" ideas often do.

Paul closed his letter to the Galatians mindful of the tensions created by his innovative, non-traditional approaches. His writing in 6:11-18 indicates that Paul had made peace with the fact that *innovation causes confrontation*—a realization that can be freeing and life-changing.

## Important Interpretations

Paul's tense rhetorical question in 3:1 reveals an unexpected harshness: "O foolish Galatians! Who has bewitched you?" This is akin to him saying: "You idiots! Who put a 'spell' on you?"

The gruffness of this comment—and many others like it—may seem uncharacteristic of a Messianic Christian leader—it sounds rather *un*-apostolic and contrary to speech bridled by Christian virtue. But before we reject one of the New Testament's principle-centered Apostles because we find him too forceful, we might want to re-examine our ideas of what constitutes acceptable "Christian" language, and make room for the need to confront stubborn people when necessary. Ministers are all-too-often asked to "be nice" and "sweet" and to never raise their voices. Was this Paul? Apparently not. Timid sorts don't change the world.

Paul *boldly wrestled* with some issues and some people and was personally *assertive*. His *forcefully contending*

# In the Footsteps of the Rabbi from Tarsus

for the essence of authentic faith and practice challenges the notion that ministers and Christians generally should "play it safe" and be politically correct, pleasing everyone in the name of a bland form of "love." Paul's behavior demonstrates that Christian preaching, teaching, and counseling should be engaging—boldly tackling the issues of the day.

If Paul's example holds any sway in our thinking, there is a place for lively and forceful dialogue in Christian communication. This does not give ministers a license to attack cherished traditions in the name of good preaching and teaching; but it does call for ministers to come to terms with their convictions and gives them a biblical precedent to voice them strongly, irrespective of the social-political climate.

Let's follow Paul's example and stand up for important issues!

In 2:1-10 we read that the other *Apostles accepted Paul's ministry and message and even endorsed both.* This is significant and worthy of some reflection, especially given the controversial nature of the man and his message.

Paul is heard taking firm stands on issues in Galatians, but he was not acting on his own; he informed his readers that he was operating under an authoritative umbrella—an "apostolic seal," if you will. Paul noted that he shared his understandings with apostolic men of repute, who extended the "right hand of fellowship."

Paul's need for others' endorsements is evident in his writing—both here and elsewhere. The process by which other leaders examined and "accredited" him is worthy of some consideration at this juncture, especially given the tendency for some to want to "go it alone" and peddle their religious ideas in the world without having them examined first by credible teachers.

If individuals now and in the past humbly presented their religious views for review before taking them to the streets, the marketplace of religious ideas would offer far less bad teaching. For that matter, isolated and remote ministers would enjoy better emotional and intellectual (not to mention spiritual) health if they were more connected to others.

Beware of those who opt to "go it alone" in their lives and ministries despite the myriad hazards. Credible pastors, preachers, academic theologians, and even scientists continually subject their ideas and theories to peer review, eliciting a variety of human critiques.

Various local church boards and denominations have processes to examine and then endorse ministers; in academia, instructors step onto their classroom podiums only after proving themselves through advanced studies under graduate-level educators.

# In the Footsteps of the Rabbi from Tarsus

In both cases, though human teachers may be imperfect, instructors being inspected and endorsed by intellectual and spiritual superiors first, guarantees a better product for their students. Would that more teachers were like Paul: *willing to humbly submit to the process of peer review* and then work within the boundaries set by legitimate authorities!

Even in the church's "rank and file," individuals can push for well-intended but misleading religious ideas that may be rooted in the creative energies of the teacher, rather than in biblical literature as interpreted by authenticated instructors. It is best that we do not tolerate this.

Though Paul placed a premium on being led "by the Spirit," it is worth noting that he was willing *not* to be led by the Spirit only. He demonstrated a willingness to submit to those humans in the "flesh" who were deemed superintendents of the Messianic movement, and who got there before he did. The notion that Paul was somehow at odds with governmental rule—in the name of "Spirit-led" living—is a mistaken assumption, and one worth calling into question. For though Paul clearly did not advocate submission to religious legislation, *he obviously did not want Believers to live without structure.*

He warned about the dangers of unbridled living, of walking in the "flesh," and advocated disciplined, virtue-led, Spirit-led living (5:16-24). He not only exhorted individuals to keep their base impulses "in check," but also asked them to place a premium on caring for others:

# Paul's Letter to the Church at Galatia

"bear one another's burdens" is the message in 6:1-5; and "given to good works" in 6:6-10. This is true religion, according to Paul; whether one keeps Jewish dietary regulations or not does not matter because such regulations do not get at the essence and substance of authentic religion.

## Contemporary Applications
How do we apply what we've learned so far? A few of my suggestions follow.

Christians need not be spineless and wimpy owing to a misconstrued sense of Christian humility and virtue. Paul took stands and spoke his mind forcefully and frankly. So should we.

Being resolute rarely produces a smooth journey, so difficulties and rejection should be anticipated as natural consequences and be borne gracefully.

Realizing this, followers of Jesus should not set out to avoid conflict and trial; rather, our purpose should be to advocate for a biblically informed worldview and prepare to gracefully absorb the resulting tensions and challenges. This is one of the lessons I gleaned from Galatians.

Though Paul was a strong-willed individual, *he wasn't a lone, strong-willed individual,* but enjoyed the support of significant allies—"accountability partners," if you will. We Americans are arguably way too autonomous. We individually minded Believers who endeavor to lead Spirit-

# In the Footsteps of the Rabbi from Tarsus

led lives might be more useful to the Lord's work if we learn to dwell and work alongside others, and to hold our peace and our place until we secure the authorization of legitimate leaders vested with the task of superintending the flock.

I've been "pushed" more than once by parishioners in churches I have led, and by students in schools where I have taught, all in the name of "the Lord is showing me such and such..." Paul did not push past legitimate superiors to give expression to his various impulses. Neither should we.

Next, Paul's premium on virtue-led living is of paramount importance, and worthy of some reflection.

Our sin-soaked society sadly lacks personal discipline and training in virtue. The call to keep the "flesh" in check and let Spirit-led, Bible-based virtue prevail is as important for Believers today as yesterday. The theologian in Paul didn't think in the abstract, didn't answer questions people weren't asking. Rather, he had a strong moral compass and required his flock to live ethically. His was a real-world theology. Paul advocated that folk not "sin," but that folk love and serve God instead.

I often think that Christian preaching would be more interesting and productive if ministers boldly challenged individuals. If they did, the church could truly be a place where people could come to ask important questions and get a handle on biblically informed moral and spiritual principles. It wouldn't be a case of someone getting offended by the minister's personality or emboldened approach, which can happen when "rites" are the goal and not "rights."

My brief Galatians assessment is hardly the final word on Paul's letter. I hope, however, that what I've "teased out" of the literature will assist other Believers to get a good read on their moral compasses, so that Christian virtue might prevail over the moral decay that is increasing its headway in our culture.

## Personal Applications

I uncovered a few issues that I find meaningful. How about you? If you've followed the suggested pathway through this book, by now you have read Paul's first letter—to the Galatians—from your Bible, and then my brief assessment of some of the issues that I find especially important. I believe that the Lord speaks to people's hearts—and not just to professional theologians—when they engage the Bible's truth. So, take a moment to reflect on that "still small voice within you" (1 Kings 19:12), and then record what you feel the Lord might be saying to you through your encounter with Paul and the Galatians. This is arguably the most important aspect of this book. In the following area, write down three points that seemed most meaningful to you and then, in narrative form, write down your ideas of how you can apply these lessons to your life.

# In the Footsteps of the Rabbi from Tarsus

Three points that seemed most meaningful to me are:

1. _____

   _____

2. _____

   _____

3. _____

   _____

The lessons I learned from the three points written above I can apply in my own life by...

_____

_____

_____

_____

_____

_____

_____

_____

_____

## 2. Paul's 1st Letter to the Church at Thessalonica

With Galatians behind us, we are now ready to consider another of Paul's letters: First Thessalonians. Paul's letter to the Galatians was prompted by false brethren troubling the church; his letter to the Thessalonians was precipitated by non-religious agitators, bent on troubling that fledgling church's members.

To maximize your personal spiritual growth and maturation, read *1 Thessalonians* now—first—then proceed with the book's overview, interpretations, and contemporary applications, which follow.

### Introductory Overview

Paul's wrote his letter to the Thessalonian Believers between 50 and 51AD, sometime during his second missionary journey. In 1:1 Paul greeted the persecuted, struggling brethren in Thessalonica and, in an encouraging manner, expressed *thanksgiving for their fellowship in the faith* (1:2-3:13); thankfulness that they'd initially received Jesus (1:2-10), reflection on his time with them (2:1-16), Timothy's glowing report of their *steadfastness* (3:2-9), and a prayer for their success (vv. 11-13).

Following his formal introduction, Paul addressed the same core values he had addressed in his letter to the Galatians. He exhorted each to *keep oneself from sin's stain* (4:1-8) and emphasized *brotherly love* (4:9-12)— the need for a righteous and kind disposition toward living Believers (being "loving")—then shifted to a consideration of deceased saints (4:13-18). He *mentioned the brethren's*

# In the Footsteps of the Rabbi from Tarsus

*being reunited and reassembled in the eschaton* (at day's end). *Eschatological readiness* (preparation for the End Times) is a theme toward the close (5:1-11), followed by general exhortations (vv. 12-22). Paul finished with a benediction (vv. 23-28).

## Important Interpretations

The opening theme of *"thanksgiving"* (1:2-10) reminds Believers that we ought to appreciate each other despite our difficulties and differences. The Church is a voluntary association, and members should not be taken for granted. Paul reminded them that he came to Thessalonica after "suffering" and after "being spitefully treated at Philippi" (2:2). The Believers there received Paul's person and his message, and became "imitators," with the result that they eventually "suffered the same things" (2:14). Shouldn't we be sensitive to the precarious nature of Christian experience and adopt an encouraging attitude toward others? Our upbeat exhortation may be the impetus that helps "put someone over the top," when they find themselves in the valley of crippling despair.

Paul's joy over their unbending, resolute *steadfastness* (3:6-8) preceded a fond recollection of his personal ministry among them, noted with a host of personal reflections. The Apostle's exhortation to *keep oneself from sin's stain* (4:1-8) indicates the pervasive and relentless nature of sin's temptation—both then and now. We will see Paul's emphasis on *keeping unsullied* from sexual sin (vv. 3-5) repeated throughout Paul's writings.

# Paul's 1<sup>st</sup> Letter to the Church at Thessalonica

Verse 8 contains a general reminder that God calls Believers to "holiness." We all should be "on guard," as sexual impulses can and do lead to ruin if not bridled and kept within the confines of sanctioned marriage. Paul's repeated theme of addressing sinfulness reminds me of Reverend Billy Graham's saying: "If there was more talking about sin in the pulpit, there would be less sin in the pew." In all his letters, Paul wrote plainly and forcefully, addressing real issues in life.

When talking of *brotherly love* Paul reminded Believers to *"mind their own business"* (4:11), and to be so *industrious professionally* that they would command the respect of outsiders (v. 12). Here again, keeping various impulses bridled seems important; but, in this case, sexual impulses aren't the issue: Keeping one's tongue in check and one's energies focused actively engages Believers in successful living and prevents them from exaggerated religious pursuits that could cause their business and social lives to languish. *Religious people can arguably become too disengaged, something that a practical-minded Paul advised against* and corrected in his epistles at every turn. But, there is a time for Christians to disengage from authentic living. When is that? At death. Until then, we must be proactive and industrious, keeping our minds focused on our primary purpose of advancing Christ's Kingdom.

Paul's belief in the resurrection of the dead, coupled with the Thessalonians' concern over departed loved ones, prompted the Apostle to address *the eventual re-*

*gathering of living and dead Believers* (4:13-18). Lest Believers focus on eschatological speculation, Paul urged a *practical state of readiness* anticipating Christ's coming. Let's not get lazy, he said in 5:6, reminding Believers to *"comfort* each other and *edify* each other," mindful of Jesus' promised return and the blessings that will accompany the moment.

## Contemporary Applications
A variety of reflection-worthy themes surface in the Thessalonian correspondence.

Though both the writer and the recipients were apparently experiencing hard times, genuine love and sincere thankfulness seem to permeate Paul's letter to the Thessalonians. We know that negative and disorienting circumstances can often prompt people to privately sink into decay, despair, and the pursuit of self-serving interests. How was Paul able to "keep his head above water?" Is there a lesson here about living and focusing our lives and energies? Paul taught that there is great merit in keeping a positive attitude even at negative times.

How do you feel around excessively negative and depressive people? Do you want to be like them, or would you prefer to keep at a distance from those with perennially negative dispositions? Granted, we all have problems, and from time to time we all need to "unload" on trusted friends. But some individuals have excessively negative dispositions that define them, day in and day out. They don't have an occasional "bad day;" they continually

# Paul's 1ˢᵗ Letter to the Church at Thessalonica

dwell on the negative and draw others into their downward spiraling dispositions. If you are affected by others' dispositions (and your own to varying degrees), and if you want to have a "victor" attitude and not a "victim" mindset, embrace the Bible's testimony that thankfulness and appreciation for others are characteristics of people with positive and maturing faith. Get a hold of this truth—you'll start moving up, not down.

An upbeat Paul closed his personal musings by saying, "may the Lord make you increase and abound in love to one another" (3:12). The Apostle believed in his congregation's ultimate success in life because faith-filled people have a better faith-filled disposition; faith-based folk are more upbeat and thankful. Modern readers of 1 Thessalonians should note this "upbeat Spirit," and be sure that it characterizes our individual Christian experience and our communal Christian experience.

Paul said that instead of being busybodies concerned with other peoples' business, we are to be "on the ready" and not wander about on the darker side of human experience. The Apostle's exhortation to *keep oneself from sin's stain* (4:1-8) and *keep unsullied* from sexual sin (vv. 3-5) addressed what were then and are now perennial problems for humans. As Paul brought these matters up time and time again, ought ministers tackle morality matters more often in exhortations and in sermons? As has been noted above and will be noted again, the Rabbi from Tarsus had a strong moral compass and was not shy about repeatedly encouraging Believers to walk worthy of God's calling. With that in mind, Christian denominations should aspire to be champions of biblical virtue, and should challenge women and men to walk uprightly and in a manner worthy of their growing Christian resolutions.

Believers should "know how to possess a marriage partner in sanctification and honor" (4:4) considering that fornication is ubiquitous in the secular culture and problematic in the Church's culture. Paul believed that beyond encouraging Christians to stay away from illicit sexual experiences, the Church should function to help single individuals find virtue-based approaches to legitimate sexual union in marriage. In many respects the Church has been lax on this score. Happily, today voices are being raised, calling individuals to consider biblical approaches to dating and courtship. This would please the Apostle Paul who wanted people to enter marriage honorably.

Benefits accrue in this life and the next to Christians in response to their stand for righteousness. There is an eventual "payday" for Believers and we all can look forward with great expectation to our rewards in Heaven. First Thessalonians contains details of Paul's belief in the resurrection—when the dead come back to life to be eternally blessed. We will see in Second Thessalonians that this doctrine was apparently a source of confusion for the Believers in Thessalonica. When and how will the dead come back to life? Is there actually a "rapture" experience? What and when is the rapture? Paul took up these questions.

# Paul's 1st Letter to the Church at Thessalonica

Despite the fascination of end-time speculation, pulling out the latest prophecy charts and fighting over how Russia, Iran, Iraq, Israel, and America might "line up" in the scheme of things may be more distractive than productive for Believers. Lest folk be preoccupied with end-time speculation—as is often the case today—we must remember that Paul placed a premium on the *practical state of readiness* in light of Jesus' eventual return. The Bible casts eschatological visions for the purpose of inspiring practical, real-world participation in the Kingdom's advancement, not to provide fodder for impractical intellectual speculation.

Much as faith without works is dead, intellectual "toots" without real-world "fruits" is problematic. Paul exhorted Believers to advance the Kingdom's interests and agendas *now*, and not sit back and wait passively for God's eventual and mysterious triumph in human history at the end of days, when life as we know it ceases and we are ushered into a new era of boundless life and prosperity.

## Personal Applications

So there you have some of my reflections on this very interesting document. What can you come up with? You have read some of what's meaningful to me. What strikes you as being especially important? If you've followed the suggested pathway through this book—and I hope and pray that you have—by now you have read 1 Thessalonians as it appears in your Bible, followed by my very brief assessment of what I consider to be the more important issues in that document. Believing that the Lord speaks

# In the Footsteps of the Rabbi from Tarsus

to people's hearts when they engage biblical truth, I have provided below a means for you to take stock of what the Lord might be saying to you. In the space that follows, write down three points that seemed most meaningful to you and then, in narrative form, write down commitment reflections on how you can apply these biblical truths.

Three points that seemed most meaningful to me are:

1. _____

_____

2. _____

_____

3. _____

_____

The lessons I learned from the three points written above I can apply in my own life by...

_____
_____
_____
_____
_____
_____

# Paul's 1st Letter to the Church at Thessalonica

## 3. Paul's 2nd Letter to the Church at Thessalonica

Having considered the Rabbi from Tarsus's first letter to the Thessalonians, you are now ready to consider his second one—a follow-up letter written shortly after the first. To maximize your personal spiritual growth and maturation, read *2 Thessalonians* now before you look at my overview, important interpretations, and contemporary applications that follow below. All the while, think about what you might personally glean from the letter, and prepare to note your reflections at the close of this section.

### Introductory Overview

Paul's second letter to the Thessalonians was written sometime between 50 and 51AD, during his second missionary journey, and apparently was penned shortly after he wrote 1 Thessalonians—perhaps only a few weeks later. This letter was comparable to the first correspondence and arguably picked-up on questions that arose from the first letter.

What precipitated its writing? We see in 1:3-4 that the Thessalonian Christians were being *persecuted* for their faith; Paul likely wrote to assure them of their eventual *triumph* and God's eventual judgment upon their foes (vv. 5-10). He reminded them of his continual prayers for them (vv. 11-12), and took up a theological issue that had caused some *confusion* among them—Bible prophecy.

As is the case today, *confusion over Bible prophecy* apparently existed in the apostolic era. Early Believers suffered severe persecution, and Paul's first letter reminding

Having dealt with the Thessalonians' "end of the world" anxieties, the Rabbi from Tarsus moved on to more "earthly" matters—a real-world tendency that is common in his epistles. He promoted the *pietistic disciplines* of prayer and love (3:1-5) and exhorted Believers to be personally industrious—that is, hardworking (vv. 6-13). Believing that the world was about to "end," *some stopped being responsible workers,* opting instead to passively await what they perceived as the imminent return of Jesus. Paul was not the least bit impressed by this misguided spirituality: "We hear that there are some who walk

# Paul's 2<sup>nd</sup> Letter to the Church at Thessalonica

them of the Lord's "second coming" caused some to think that their present troubles indicated that they were living at the "ragged edge of time" during the "Tribulation Period," and that they had somehow missed the "Lord's Day"—noted in 1 Thessalonians—as a result. In response, Paul wrote and corrected the erroneous notion that the "Day" had come and gone without them (2:1-2), after which he explained the necessary precedents to the end of the era.

What will transpire in advance of the Kingdom's final coming? A *rebellion* comes (v. 3a), followed by an *antiChrist* (vv. 3b-5). Then the "wicked one" is restrained (vv. 6-7), but his doom is eventual (v. 8). After Paul told about the antiChrist's deceitfulness (vv. 9-12), he reminded them that *those who become saints will prevail* though they be tormented (vv. 13-14). Paul said that Believers will have the grace to "*stand firm*" (v. 15). Paul closed the point with a benediction (vv. 16-17).

among you in a disorderly manner, not working at all but are busybodies" (v. 11). Paul's response: work! he said forcefully (v. 12). If they didn't—because of some misguided, other-worldly spirituality—Paul recommended a firm rebuke (v. 14). He then closed his letter.

## Important Interpretations

Paul felt prompted to write an immediate follow-up to his first letter, given concerns over the possibility that the Thessalonians' had misunderstood his stance on Bible prophecy and the Church's position in the "last days." This only underscores how confusing the subject really was back then—and still is today. It is easy for us to identify with the early Believers' conviction that they were living in the End Times. In hindsight, we can see the error in their thinking and the wisdom of Paul's stern rebuke to the misguided spiritual prophecy experts who quit working to await the end of the world. Paul referred to these prophecy interpreters as "disorderly" (3:11). Many today believe that *we* are living in the End Times, just as many generations over the past 2,000 years believed *they* were living in the End Times. Therefore, Paul's instructions to the early Christians—to continue to live responsibly and advance the Kingdom—apply equally to us, lest future generations look back similarly on us. We can also learn from Paul's exhortation to the more-balanced brethren to be sympathetic toward the disengaged members (v. 15). In v. 14, however, he told the Church—and us—to resist the dangerous doctrines and habits advocated by these unsteady, speculative, and lazy souls. *Paul advocated for responsible living.*

# Paul's 2<sup>nd</sup> Letter to the Church at Thessalonica

The Thessalonians' persecution reminds us afresh that *bad things can and do happen to good people.* Though they were buffeted with "trials," Paul reminded them—and us by extension—that help for the righteous is on the way; for there is a God who will "repay with tribulation those who trouble" the saints (1:6). At the same time, the tendency for suffering Christians to misinterpret their difficult condition and construe their dire circumstances as evidence that they have "missed God" or have displeased Him is worth addressing. Apparently the Thessalonian Believers did just that, and Paul wanted to correct their misunderstanding. The challenges and tests, he said, are not evidence of God's disfavor, as some thought; to the contrary, they are vehicles to enable Believers to be "counted worthy of this calling," and serve to help Christians "fulfill all the good pleasure of God's goodness" (v. 11).

Though there will be a devil-inspired "falling away" amidst this turmoil and distress (2:3a), Paul voiced his confidence that these Thessalonian Believers would not be unduly influenced, even though they were misguided by popular misunderstandings. "We are bound to give thanks for you brethren," he said (v. 13) and then declared that the Thessalonians "will obtain the glory of the Lord Jesus Christ" (v. 14). Here again, Paul's faith believed and hoped all things for the brethren. We should all aspire to have similar faith, even amidst life's difficult circumstances!

# In the Footsteps of the Rabbi from Tarsus

Paul's general appeal for prayer and love (3:1-2) and his note that they should "withdraw from every brother who walks disorderly" (3:6), reminds us of the general *tension between truth and grace,* on the one hand, and the particular *problem associated with misguided religious zeal* on the other. Though sympathetic, Paul was not impressed by the "heavenly minded" Believers; for *Paul preferred that Believers live constructive lives* in anticipation of Christ's coming, rather than live nonproductively, certain that His arrival is imminent. We need to heed Paul's words.

## Contemporary Applications

Prophecy students find 2 Thessalonians to be very informative and intellectually engaging. Therein, one hears Paul speaking of the antiChrist, of a last days rebellion, of Believers in peril, and of social upheaval that attends all of the above. The fantastic verbiage comes filled with themes of agony and ecstasy. Believers' precarious place in the unfolding drama guarantees that the Thessalonian passage will be the center of conversation and controversy for quite some time. Given the difficulties associated with interpreting eschatological literature, grounded interpreters are wise to proceed cautiously—if for no other reason than to avoid making the same mistake the Thessalonians made through their overzealousness. Considering all that is involved—pain, suffering, release from incessant oppression, rewards, and punishments—some will be passionate about their "end of the world" views. Still, passionate and dogmatic souls run the risk of falling into the trap that Paul wanted the Thessalonians to avoid: being too heavenly minded at the expense of being of no earthly good.

Paul seemed to believe that not everyone would hear him out, and he told his audience to identify, to rebuke, and to disassociate with those "disorderly" spirits who wouldn't submit to his apostolic authority. The tendency for "spiritually minded" people to think they "know better" and need not submit to legitimate Church authorities was a problem then, much as it is a problem now—especially among folk who believe that they see what God is up to, while others miss it. Newer Believers seem more apt to chase after personal prophecies and anxiously attend prophecy conferences than more mature Believers. When the enthusiasm runs its course, it's all about settling down and working together to advance Christ's Kingdom together—alongside those vested with legitimate biblical authority to lead the sacred enterprise.

Paul seemed not to have been especially concerned—as some of the Thessalonians were—that they would somehow miss Christ's coming. His concern was that they might miss what God would have them do on Earth, prior to His arrival—because of bad theology rooted in bad eschatology. He was also concerned that the Believers would be unnecessarily troubled emotionally and intellectually because of the bad theology. *We'd all do well to guard against bad teaching*—though it might sound spectacular when we hear it. It is better for us to focus our energies on right living, now. Let's not be overly concerned—to the detriment of our souls—with the timing of the coming new era when Christ makes His entrance afresh onto the stage of the human drama; but let's invest our energies and resources in advancing the Kingdom of our Lord and of His Christ while it is yet "day." Those so inclined will get an affirmation from Paul in Heaven. He may well say to us: "Hey, I see you read my writings and took them to heart."

## Personal Applications

So much for my reflections. What's on your mind? If you've followed the suggested pathway through this book, you will have read the biblical letter, followed by my reflections on what I consider some of the more important issues in Paul's second letter to the Thessalonians. Now, let the Lord speak to you and take stock of what He says. In the space provided, write down three points that seemed most meaningful to you and then, in narrative form, write down ideas on how you can apply these biblical truths.

Three points that seemed most meaningful to me are:

1. _____

   _____

2. _____

   _____

# Paul's 2nd Letter to the Church at Thessalonica

3. _____

_____

The lessons I learned from the three points written above I can apply in my own life by....

_____

_____

_____

_____

_____

_____

_____

_____

_____

_____

_____

_____

_____

## 4. Paul's 1st Letter to the Church at Corinth

We now consider one of Paul's major epistles: First Corinthians. To maximize your personal spiritual growth and maturation, read *1 Corinthians* now—before reading my overview, important interpretations, and contemporary applications.

### Introductory Overview

Paul wrote First Corinthians in approximately 55AD, during his third missionary journey. There is textual evidence that Paul got word from a noteworthy source that *troubles were abounding* in the fledgling Corinthian church, which he had spent eighteen months laboring to establish. In the wake of his formal salutations, Paul noted the report given to him, and proceeded to address the church's *divisions* and reports of *immorality* and *fighting among members.* As vexing as these were, this was only the beginning salvo. Reports of *sexual improprieties* troubled Paul greatly, prompting him to elaborate on *marriage,* being *single,* and the like. Questions about what could be eaten prompted Paul to address food concerns in the context of which he urged *consideration* toward Christians with differing perspectives on these and other non-essential issues. He wrote about re-establishing the *order of public worship* including appropriate dress, communion rites, and *"spiritual gifts."* *Love's precedence* preceded a reminder about the proper employment of *ecstatic utterances*—with "checks and balances." After speaking on utterances, Paul gave voice to a correct understanding of the *doctrine of the resurrection* of the dead. Paul closed the hefty letter with an instruction for a *planned financial contribution* to the Jerusalem saints, talk of Timothy's coming visit, Apollos' failure to come, greetings, and commendations.

## Important Interpretations

Reports of internal *troubles* precipitated Paul's first letter to the Corinthians, reminding us that *churches are not perfect societies.* We may wish they were; but, in truth, they never were, and never will be.

In Corinth, many were possessed with sectarian spirits and divided around different leadership personalities (1:10-17). Some preferred Peter's leadership, others preferred Paul's; some were inclined toward Apollos' erudite presentations, whereas others mistakenly thought that being "led by the Spirit" meant no contact whatsoever with any human agency. Unimpressed by divisiveness parading around in the guise of some superior brand of spirituality, Paul referred to the insidious sectarianism as "carnality [in the guise of spirituality]" (3:1-4). He preferred that authorized spiritual leaders *work together* for the advancement of the Kingdom (vv. 5-17). In 4:1-5, the Rabbi from Tarsus explained that teachers were "stewards of God's mysteries" and should not be rated against each another.

Though the Corinthians may have had "ten thousand instructors," they did "not have many fathers" (4:15). Whether or not they saw him as a father, Paul, the actual founder of the church (humanly speaking), saw himself as their father. Displeased by their poor performance, he

# In the Footsteps of the Rabbi from Tarsus

said—much like a father—that he would come to his children either with a "rod" or with a spirit of "gentleness" to correct the problems. It was up to them, which. In Second Corinthians we will see that he opted for the former first and followed, when possible, with leniency.

After dealing with *divisions* around preferred spiritual guides and personalities, Paul addressed the fact that members of the church were at odds with each other, even taking out *lawsuits* against each other. He expressed dismay that Christian brothers were taking other Believers to court (6:1) rather than allowing other, more mature Believers to judge and settle the contested matters through the church's leadership. He saw their actions as "an utter failure" on their part (v. 7), flying in the face of what Jesus would have Believers do and be.

The lack of social control indicated the lack of personal control in other areas. Reports of *sexual improprieties* disturbed Paul. In 5:1, Paul noted that someone was committing immorality at a level that would make even the heathen blush—no easy task, given the rife sexual impropriety in Corinthian culture. Paul pointed out the need to discipline the lapsed person in order that "the one who has done this deed might be taken away" (v. 2). Paul ordered the man's temporary removal from the community, noting how "a little leaven leavens the whole lump" (v. 6) and commanded the community to "purge out the old leaven" (v. 7). *Paul confronted problems that others seemed to ignore.*

# Paul's 1ˢᵗ Letter to the Church at Corinth

Paul wrote explicitly in vv. 9-12 lest his poetic language be misunderstood: "I wrote you [previously] in my epistle not to keep company with sexually immoral people"; and to this he added in v. 11, "But now I have written to you not to keep company with anyone named a brother, who is sexually immoral, or covetous, or an idolater, or a reviler, or a drunkard, or an extortioner—not even to eat with such a person." Paul told us in 6:19, "the body is the temple of the Holy Spirit" and, as such, is defiled if one "keeps company with a harlot" (v. 16). In conjunction with his hard-line approach to sexual impropriety and carnal indulgences, Paul also discussed legitimate, God-sanctioned outlets for sexual expression: "Because of sexual immorality, it is good for each man to have his own wife, and let each woman have her own husband" (7:2).

Couples were encouraged to submit to each other's needs and interests (vv. 3-5), and were instructed to not "deprive each other sexually" (v. 5). Paul dealt with human nature's tendencies toward marriage dissolution (vv. 10-16), advocating for union over disunion. Though Paul was unmarried—at least at this point in his life—he understood that this wasn't the norm for all people; for "if you do marry you have not sinned," he said (v. 28).

Paul moved beyond these sexual and relational matters and addressed the need for *consideration* toward Christians with differing perspectives on non-essential doctrines in 8:1-11:1. Though Paul was inflexible on morality, he encouraged Christian liberty in non-essential domains. In chapter 8, for example, Paul dealt with dietary decisions and left food consumption to individual conscience. This contrasted directly with members of the "circumcision party" who mandated adherence to Jewish dietary regulations. Paul believed that unity—though very important to him—need not be purchased with enforced uniformity in every religious practice. Paul had his preferences—his essentials—and knew how and when to stand firm with them. He apparently knew how to bend as well, and was not minded to govern every aspect of other people's lives. Would that we were as flexible and tolerant!

Re-establishing the *order of public worship* was important to Paul (chapters 11-14). For the same reasons debated today, head coverings were an issue in Paul's day (11:2-16). For whatever reason, Paul dug in his heals on this point, firmly saying that he would accept no other practice (v. 16). Might he have been pushing here for a contrast between Christian practices and neighboring pagan ones? Perhaps (see Roman rules in footnote #2 in Chapter 1).

Paul's concern can also be observed in his statements regarding the "Lord's Supper," a meal that the Corinthians were apparently defiling with an insensitive disregard for poorer Believers.

After discussing the Communion tradition in 11:23-26, Paul noted that people were defiling themselves, bringing judgment upon themselves, and making themselves unfit for the Supper because they did not examine themselves properly, first (vv. 27-32). The real issue may be obscured, as with the issue of head coverings. Paul noted "the hungry should eat at home, lest you come together for judgment" (v. 34). They were divided along caste or class lines, and because Communion typically came at the end of a fellowship supper, the wealthier Believers apparently ate the "pot luck" food staples before the poorer Believers could get served. This invoked the ire of the Rabbi from Tarsus. As we have seen, Paul was not impressed by social systems that differentiated between the rich and the poor, seeing these systems as the very antithesis of the Christian faith and virtue he was advocating.

Beyond the Corinthians' misuse of social prestige, as reflected in the misuse of food staples, Paul worried about their use and possible misuse of *"spiritual gifts."* Just after his introduction (1:1-3), Paul had noted that the Corinthians were "enriched" with "all utterance and knowledge" (v. 5), and that they lacked "no gift" (v. 7). Because he indicated a dissatisfaction with the theological and structural chaos in the church, he may have been speaking tongue-in-cheek there. At any rate, the use of spiritual gifts mattered to Paul.

In chapter 12, Paul noted how, like a human body, the "body of Christ" has many parts. He discussed diversities of *gifts* of the Spirit (vv. 4 and 8-11), diversities of formal *roles* (vv. 12-27), and diversities of church *government*—

# In the Footsteps of the Rabbi from Tarsus

these being "apostles, prophets, teachers, miracle [workers], gifts of healings, helps, administrators, administrations," and then lastly "varieties of tongues" (vv. 27-28). Not all possess all of these gifts (vv. 29-30); Paul seemed content that Believers are gifted differently, but he insisted that we all share the greatest gift: love—*the loving of one Believer for the other.* Paul postulated that the core values of *love and consideration* must remain constant.

Though often employed at weddings, the "love chapter"— 1 Corinthians 13—is really more about brotherly love and congregational love, than the love of a man and a woman. "Though I speak in the tongues of men and angels" (v. 1) refers to spiritual gifts at work in corporate gatherings, and *not* the dialogue of a married couple. The phrase "If I have the gift of prophecy, and understand all mysteries and knowledge" (v. 2) speaks of "gifts," as does the later mention that "we know in part and we prophesy in part" (v. 9). After saying in v. 12 that, at best, we all "see dimly," Paul noted that the greatest characteristic and gift of all is "love" (v. 13). If we stretch it far enough we can apply this chapter to marriage, but providing wedding material was not the passage's primary purpose. Paul never conducted a wedding—nor did any Apostle of record—and there is no indication that he was minded to do so when he put pen to paper to write this epistle. Paul was interested in Christians getting along in the increasingly divisive Corinthian church. This was the situation he was addressing.

# Paul's 1st Letter to the Church at Corinth

If "speaking in tongues" was the litmus test to judge spirituality, then the Corinthians were truly in great shape; for as Paul noted in the introduction, they seemed to abound with many ecstatic, spiritual gifts. They also seemed to have abundant problems with gross sexual immorality, problems with theological divisiveness and jealousies among the Believers, problems enough to take each other to court, problems with Communion, and even heretical doctrine (see the misunderstanding of the resurrection in chapter 15), all of which seem to indicate that *"speaking in tongues" is not the best test to assess one's spiritual temperature.* Even today, some Christians make this mistake—and what a horrible one it is. They seem to think that if someone "speaks in tongues," all is well. This shallow notion cannot stand after even a casual reading of this Pauline epistle and should be replaced by more mature approaches to assessing the Christian life.

Could Paul's telling them to "pursue love" while still "desiring spiritual gifts" (14:1) be significant? Paul was pleased that folk spoke in "tongues" (v. 5), something he said that he did as well (v. 18)—and all the time. He noted, however, that "since you are zealous for spiritual gifts, let it be for the edification of the church that you seek to excel" (vv. 12-13). Mindful of this, and wanting all Believers to benefit from God-sent ecstatic utterances, Paul advocated for an "interpretation" (v. 13): "I thank my God [that] I speak with tongues more than you all; yet

181

in the church I would rather speak five words with my understanding, that I may teach others also, than ten thousand words in a tongue" (vv. 18-19).

All in all, for Paul, love's charm took precedence over the charm of spectacular, outward charismatic gifts. Though personally in possession of various spiritual gifts, Paul advocated for the proper employment of those gifts in corporate gatherings, wanting "checks and balances" on the *ecstatic utterances* that he seemed to greatly cherish.

After speaking on spiritual utterances, Paul explained a correct understanding of the *doctrine of the resurrection* of the dead in chapter 15. Even with their spiritual gifts, the Corinthians were so close, yet so far away. Paul was beside himself with grief when he moved on to his next subject: their misunderstanding of basic and essential Christian doctrine. He rhetorically asked: "If Christ is preached that He was raised from the dead, how do some among you say that there is no resurrection?" (15:12). His question—what was really an opening statement—came on the heels of his saying, "I delivered to you as of first importance what I also received, that Christ died for our sins according to the Scriptures, and that He was buried and that He rose again the third day according to the Scriptures" (vv. 3-4). His emphasis on "according to the Scriptures" indicates that he wanted them to accept this understanding on biblical authority and not simply on his apostolic authority—an authority that wasn't universally accepted and was even being challenged by some at Corinth. The Apostle cogently

# Paul's 1st Letter to the Church at Corinth

developed the argument for the resurrection, ending with "Therefore, my beloved brethren, be steadfast, immovable, always abounding in the work of the Lord, knowing that your labor is not in vain in the Lord" (v. 58).

On the heels of addressing the need to be "steadfast in the work of the Lord," and after correcting poor practice and doctrine in this rather lengthy "major" epistle, Paul closed with instructions for the *planned financial contribution* to the Jerusalem saints (16:10-24), a matter that we will view in more detail in his second correspondence. Even with everything that was happening in this church, Paul thought to encourage them to be good financial stewards and to bless others.

## Contemporary Applications

Many applications can be drawn from this letter, said to be a "casebook in pastoral theology." My samplings:

This letter being prompted by reports of *trouble* in the Corinthian community underscores a point that dissatisfied church members need to remember: *church communities made up of real-world, everyday people are not perfect societies. We do well to temper our idealism with some grace and realism.* Human nature being what it is, perfection is not going to be achieved this side of the grave. *Attempting* to be more perfect in conduct, however, is both achievable and expected; fleshly attitudes and conduct are to be eschewed.

# In the Footsteps of the Rabbi from Tarsus

*Division* around religious leadership personalities was problematic—then and now. Should the Church of Jesus Christ be a personality cult? No. Should charismatic ministers be adored like rock stars? Of course not! However, it happens—to the detriment of both the minister and his congregants. In the Corinthian world, people compared and contrasted leaders. The result was that some preferred Peter's leadership, others preferred Paul's, and some took a special liking to Apollos' style. Still others—caring little for any human leadership at all—were said to have responded only to Christ, and thus only to the Spirit's leading. The Rabbi from Tarsus criticized the entire process, seeing it as sectarian and carnal—and not spiritual at all. Would that we all were so minded!

Comparing oneself to others is arguably a human inclination—and an oppressive one at that. It is not a helpful characteristic for those trying to cultivate a godly nature. How many women and men become depressed by comparing themselves to others? Way too many! Paul preferred that authorized spiritual leaders *work together* to advance the Kingdom, a habit we should all adopt. Paul said that, collectively, teachers are "stewards of God's mysteries" and shouldn't be compared and "judged" against one another.

After dealing with divisions brought on by preferences for spiritual guides and charismatic personalities, Paul took on the fact that members of the church were taking out *lawsuits* against each other (6:1-11) and he counted

# Paul's 1ˢᵗ Letter to the Church at Corinth

this as "an utter failure" on their part. Do Christians today look to settle grievances first, or do we instead run to the courts for redress? The Church is to be a reconciling community. Though seen by others as a failure of the Gospel, it's not the Gospel that fails; rather, it's our inability to resolve tensions that diminishes our demonstration of the Gospel's healing power, and thus we lose our opportunity to witness. Better that we find ways to reconcile and discover new ways to live at peace with others.

Paul saw the lack of social controls as an indicator that personal control in other areas—hidden areas—was lacking. His concern about reports of *sexual improprieties* and his willingness to confront problems that others seemed predisposed to ignore serve as examples that we are not to be sheepish about confronting issues and people when necessary—for their good and the community's.

Paul was not against sexuality but frowned upon illicit heterosexual sexual contact. *For Paul, individuals should not have sexual contact without a contract*—a marriage contract. Enjoying the pleasures of sexuality without protecting the treasures of sexuality—the children—is irresponsible, to put it mildly. "It is good for each man to have his own wife, and let each woman have her own husband," he said in 7:2. Within the confines of a covenant contract, couples were encouraged to submit to each other's needs and interests, and were told to not "deprive each other sexually." Requiring that a binding contract be in place to legitimize sexual expression between partners meant that all other heterosexual arrangements were to be eschewed, as were homosexual ones outright.

Paul's correspondence about the need for *consideration* toward Christians with differing perspectives on non-essential doctrines contrasts his inflexibility on morality matters with flexibility on non-essential matters—an adroitness we would do well to embrace. We should be as flexible, and not push our opinions on others, especially on non-essential matters. Pushy people think themselves mature; though the inclination to impose their beliefs on others actually advertises to the world what children they really are.

Paul's section on re-establishing the *order of public worship* reminds us that there must be structure to public services. We shouldn't abandon structure in the name of spirituality—as the Corinthians did. Paul's angst over the abuse of the "Lord's Supper," where some were insensitive to the poorer Believers, reminds us that discriminating in favor of wealthier members of the congregation at the expense of those less fortunate offends the Gospel!

Concerns over social abuses led to concerns about spiritual misuse. Though Paul prized spiritual gifts, he placed his personal premium on proven character over personal charisma. By instructing the Corinthians to "pursue love" while still "desiring spiritual gifts," the Apostle was counseling the Corinthians to correct their myriad

# Paul's 1st Letter to the Church at Corinth

deficiencies, recover their spiritual equilibrium, and restore their relationship with each other and with him.

## Personal Applications

Now that you have some of my "two cents" on First Corinthians let me ask you to put down some of yours. You can be a theologian too! If you've followed the suggested pathway through this book, by this point you have read the biblical Text followed by my brief assessment of some of the more important issues in the first Corinthian correspondence. Now let the Lord speak to your heart and use the space provided below as a means for you to take stock of what the Lord might be saying to you. Write down three points that seemed most meaningful to you and then in narrative form, write down how you can apply these biblical truths.

Three points that seemed most meaningful to me are:

1. _____

_____

_____

2. _____

_____

_____

# In the Footsteps of the Rabbi from Tarsus

3. _____

   _____

   _____

The lessons I learned from the three points written above
I can apply in my own life by…

_____
_____
_____
_____
_____
_____
_____
_____
_____
_____
_____
_____
_____
_____
_____
_____
_____

# Paul's 2<sup>nd</sup> Letter to the Church at Corinth

## Paul's 2<sup>nd</sup> Letter to the Church at Corinth

In First Corinthians, Paul was fighting a "battle royal," and the outcome was not altogether certain when he put pen to paper. Would the divided community listen to him in the controversy, or to the other factions bent on marginalizing and minimizing him? Would the Corinthians hear Paul out and discipline the recalcitrant sinner guilty of heinous sexual improprieties, or would they keep a casual attitude toward sexual sin? Would they amend other defects in their church, or would they be hard-hearted? These questions plagued Paul, whose control was being eroded even as he wrote. By the time he wrote his second letter to the Corinthians, however, these matters seem to have been resolved—and in his favor. As we shall see, Paul was on better footing with his flock when he wrote the second epistle, and he was pleased to learn that they had accepted his correction and were working to remedy deficient situations accordingly. To enhance your understanding of this epistle, and to maximize your personal spiritual growth and maturation, read *2 Corinthians* now—before reading my overview, important interpretations, and contemporary applications. Doing so will make the following reflections more meaningful.

## Introductory Overview

Paul wrote his second letter to the Corinthians during his third missionary journey, in approximately 56AD. After formally greeting the brethren, he affirmed his relationship with the church—a relationship that was tragically and seriously in question when he wrote First Corinthians.

# In the Footsteps of the Rabbi from Tarsus

He expressed thanksgiving for comfort and protection, explained his failure to visit them, and gave them *instructions for restoring the brother* who had fallen into *sexual immorality*, the one arguably mentioned in 1 Corinthians 5:1. Paul shared miscellaneous reflections on his life and *his relationship to the Corinthians* with pleas for them to be *separate from unbelievers*. Then he expressed great joy that the majority of Corinthians had, apparently, *reaffirmed their support for him.*

The Rabbi from Tarsus wrote and exhorted the newly reconciled Believers to *contribute toward the offering* for the Messianic Jews in Jerusalem, an issue he broached in his first epistle. Feeling more secure in his relationship with the Corinthians at this juncture, Rabbi Paul was confident enough to "raise" an offering. Then the Apostle turned his attention to the minority who were still at odds with him. Boldly, he took a stand against charges of personal cowardice and asserted his patriarchal claim. With *fatherly affection* and concern, he expressed continual *concern over false teachers* and defended himself, affirming his love for them and proving it by not taking money from them.

Paul then *boasted of his sufferings*—to draw attention to his commitment—and noted challenges that he had faced for the Messiah's sake and theirs. He reminded the Corinthians that *God was with him, evident in the signs and wonders* in his ministry. He announced a coming visit and offered a farewell benediction and a closing exhortation.

# Paul's 2<sup>nd</sup> Letter to the Church at Corinth

## Important Interpretations

Paul's instructions in 2:5-11, on *restoring the brother who had fallen into sexual immorality*, merit some reflection. Paul had been firm in 1 Corinthians 5:1. Then, with reports that indicated sincere repentance on the part of the previously recalcitrant and immoral person, Paul seemed inclined to suggest the church not be "too severe" with the fellow (v. 5). The punishment had apparently been "sufficient for such a man" (v. 6). Based on information that the situation was being remedied, Paul said that they "ought rather to [now] forgive and comfort him, lest perhaps such a one be swallowed up with too much sorrow...I urge you to reaffirm your love to him" (v. 7-8). This is refreshing and an added corrective for those who see Paul as too mean. Paul rebuked individuals to correct them, but once their conduct was amended, Paul softened. Would that we were so inclined, and prudent in our management of the errant!

While harking to the need to reaffirm the now-repentant fellow, Paul was mindful that the collective church had reconnected with him, Paul; now, in Second Corinthians, Paul was minded to reconnect with them, believing that he was on better footing with them socially and spiritually. At the time of First Corinthians, Paul's authority was in question, given the community's tendency to listen to a variety of leaders—Paul being but one, and a questionable one at that. Now, though, they apparently had happily come back under his tutelage in response to his previous efforts, prompting Paul to adopt a kinder approach in writing Second Corinthians.

# In the Footsteps of the Rabbi from Tarsus

Paul reflected on *his relationship with the Corinthians* (2:12-6:10). Some said he was the "aroma of death" (2:16); by contrast, others—and the Corinthians now too, apparently—perceived Paul as "the fragrance of God's knowledge" (v. 14), "of Christ" (v. 15), and the "aroma of life (v. 16). Though he appreciated the turn of affections his way, Paul said he did not "want to commend himself" (3:1); he did want to note that the Corinthians themselves were his "epistle," with God's Word written on their hearts through his ministry (vv. 2-3)—an understanding they apparently were reminded of and had sufficiently reaffirmed. In 4:1-11 Paul talked about his ministry "not to commend" himself (5:12), but to give the Corinthians an "opportunity to boast on Paul's behalf." Apparently slandered previously, Paul cast a vision for himself as a legitimate "worker together with Christ" (6:1), "as a minister of God in patience, in tribulations, in needs, in distresses, in stripes, imprisonments" (vv. 4-10), and he emotionally appealed to them saying, "O Corinthians! We have spoken openly to you, our heart is wide open..." (v. 11), and, "Open your hearts to us. We have wronged no one, we have corrupted no one, we have cheated no one" (7:2). After this emotional appeal, Paul expressed great joy over Titus' report to him that the Corinthians had reaffirmed him (vv. 13-16). Back in the "driver's seat," Paul exhorted the Believers to *contribute toward the offering* for the Messianic Jews in Jerusalem (8:1-9:15).

Paul's popular declaration that "the Lord loves a cheerful giver" (2 Corinthians 9:6-7) is often misunderstood.

# Paul's 2<sup>nd</sup> Letter to the Church at Corinth

Though often employed by local church leaders to exhort the faithful *in* the local church to financially support endeavors *in* or *for* the local church, this passage was *not* written with that sort of stewardship in mind—but it works for local church giving nevertheless. Paul was raising "mission money," to assist Jewish Believers in Jerusalem in particular; in this connection we hear him exhorting non-Jewish Believers to marshal some of their meager financial resources (which they had been indeed hard-pressed to acquire), to show their support for the beleaguered brethren in Judea.

In 2 Corinthians chapter 8, Paul harked back to the Macedonian churches' "liberal" financial support (v. 2), and reminded folk in the Corinthian suburb of Achaia that Jesus "became poor" (v. 9) in order to bless folk and make them rich. Then he encouraged the Corinthians to fulfill their financial obligation saying, "you must complete the doing of it" (vv. 10-11) in order that "your abundance may supply their lack" (v. 14).

Who was suffering the lack? Not wanting to chance lackluster results from the offering, Paul said that he had "boasted" in Macedonia of their willingness to give and that he had, in effect, used their example to "stir up" others there to assist (9:2). Should they not deliver on their promise of financial support, his apostolic ministry would be tarnished—something he was anxious to avoid. Why was Paul trying to "stir up" others to contribute? *He wanted to raise an offering to assist Jewish Believers in Judea.*

# In the Footsteps of the Rabbi from Tarsus

In 10:1-11, Paul delineated the scope of his apostolic authority. He wanted to operate "within the limits of the sphere" of influence (v. 13), and was concerned that he not be perceived as "overextending his authority" (v. 14), or operating "beyond his measure" (v. 15). In this letter he had no reservations about expressing his "jealousy" over false fathers inclined to seduce the Corinthians away and out from under Paul's influence (11:1-4). "I am not the least bit inferior to those most eminent [so-called] apostles," an emboldened Paul said (v. 5); besides, "these are false prophets, deceitful workers, transforming themselves as apostles of Christ" (v. 13). Paul was within his right to speak thusly; the false apostles, by contrast, had no right to undermine his authority as they had been doing.

In 12:11-13, Paul reminded his audience that *God was with him, evident in the signs and wonders worked through his ministry.* The Corinthian Believers placed a very high premium on spiritual gifts and considered them criteria to authenticate competing ministries. Understanding this, Paul related personal supernatural experiences in 12:1-6, claiming that supernatural gifts were in evidence through him: "the signs of an apostle were done among you... in signs and wonders and mighty deeds," in verses 11-13. Paul was not inferior to his adversaries, who claimed that he was.

## Contemporary Applications
The Rabbi from Tarsus wanted to *restore the brother* who had fallen into *sexual immorality.* This is worthy of

# Paul's 2<sup>nd</sup> Letter to the Church at Corinth

significant reflection, especially given ubiquitous problems with sexual impropriety in our culture today—in both the Church and society at large. In dealing with the matter of sexual impropriety, yesterday, Paul was firm—a trademark of his; still, when he observed sincere repentance, Paul became more kindly disposed. Instructions for exclusion yielded to a course of reconciliation for the man and his estranged community.

Paul softened his tone when speaking of the need to reaffirm the fellow. The church had recently reconnected with Paul and he wanted to make that connection a secure one. Today, Paul is considered the decisive authority for Christian faith and practice—the prominence of his writing in the New Testament signals his esteemed position—yet, in his own day and time, Paul was not appreciated universally in all the churches, and even the congregations founded by him tended to be unstable in their support for him. This shifting dynamic underscores the precariousness of ministerial experience, where support can erode quickly.

We see a lack of pastor support in many sectors of the Christian Church. Approximately twenty-five percent of local church ministers are eventually fired from their posts. The number of unhappy departures would be higher if we factored in the pastors who changed churches because of discontentment behind the scenes. Not wanting to part amid expressions of anger and disappointment, congregations and pastors settle for "The Lord has led brother so-and-so to another assignment." This

# In the Footsteps of the Rabbi from Tarsus

sanitized version often obscures the harsher realities: that the transition can be attributed to unresolved bitterness and frustration, more often associated with professional rejections than with anything else. *Perhaps we should labor to do a better job of supporting our spiritual leaders.*

A reconnected and reaffirmed Paul talked about his ministry, "not to commend" himself (5:12) but to give the Corinthians an "opportunity to boast on Paul's behalf." Though slandered by others, Paul asserted here that he was a legitimate "worker" (6:1), noting that he was "a minister of God in patience, in tribulations, in needs, in distresses, in stripes, imprisonments" (vv. 4-10). At first, the reader is reminded that ministry is full of challenges, as is the Christian life. *What demon in hell ever suggested that the Christian life was to be devoid of a Cross, and measured by boundless experiences of personal peace and affluence?* This was not Jesus' experience, nor was it Paul's. Though it might exist in the popular imaginations and sermons of some prosperity preachers, bent on raising funds for themselves, it wasn't the experience of our first spiritual leaders—certainly not Paul. We ought to reject easy-living theologies as incongruous with biblical Christianity.

What of his fundraising? Paul exhorted the Believers to *contribute toward an offering* (8:1-9:15). The Apostle was raising mission and benevolence funds from non-Jewish Believers in Corinth to assist Jewish Believers in Jerusalem. We hear him exhorting the church to marshal financial resources in order to show their support for the beleaguered brethren in Judea. Paul said that he "boasted" in Macedonia of their willingness to give and had used their example to "stir up" others to assist (9:2).

Shouldn't the Church assist with advancing the Kingdom among Jewish people—and all people? Those wanting to walk in the footsteps of the Apostle Paul—who took his lead from Jesus—need to recover an emphasis on reaching out to the "lost sheep of the house of Israel"—following the Bible's instruction and example—and to set missions giving as a priority. Paul urged Christians to be so minded.

In 10:1-11, Paul delineated the scope of his apostolic authority, and noted his resolve to operate "within the limits of the sphere" (v. 13). If we followed Paul's example, we'd spend less time getting into other people's business, what my counselor/psychologist wife calls "boundary violations." Busybodies and false brethren seem determined to draw attention to what's wrong with other people—faults that might be somewhat true or completely imagined. In either case, the spirit working within the process tends to fragment faith and resolution, and thus advances individuals' own agendas rather than the Kingdom's. Paul felt forced to say: "I am not the least bit inferior to those most eminent [so-called] apostles" (11:5), after which he noted "these are false prophets, deceitful workers, transforming themselves as apostles of Christ" (v. 13). May we be on guard against those who break up Christian unity and community for purposes of their own personal gain!

# In the Footsteps of the Rabbi from Tarsus

Paul claimed that *God was with him, evidenced by the signs and wonders.* What a difference from today's world where spiritual gifts are disbelieved and denigrated. We see that supernatural giftings were part of Pauline Christianity when Paul noted that "the signs of an apostle were done among you...in signs and wonders and mighty deeds" (12:11-13). While granting that not all Believers will speak in tongues or place a premium on spiritual gifting, we remember that *charismatic experience was part of apostolic experience, and is clearly demonstrated in the New Testament.* Paul placed a premium on gifts; perhaps we should make room for God's mysterious workings in our lives.

## Personal Applications

If you've followed the suggested pathway through this book, by this point you have read the biblical Text followed by my brief assessment of some of the more important issues in the second Corinthian correspondence. Now let the Lord speak to your heart and use the space provided below to take stock of what the Lord says to you. Write down three points that seemed most meaningful to you and then in narrative form, write down how you can apply these biblical truths.

Three points that seemed most meaningful to me are:

1. _____

_____

# Paul's 2<sup>nd</sup> Letter to the Church at Corinth

2. _____

   _____

3. _____

   _____

The lessons I learned from the three points written above
I can apply in my own life by…

_____

_____

_____

_____

_____

_____

_____

_____

_____

_____

_____

_____

_____

# In the Footsteps of the Rabbi from Tarsus

## 6. Paul's Letter to the Christians in Rome

To maximize your personal spiritual growth and maturation, read *Romans* now—before reading my overview, interpretations, and contemporary applications.

**Introductory Overview**

Paul was not the founding pastor of the church at Rome; and when he wrote the Roman epistle, Paul had not yet visited the church. Why then did he write to the Romans? Not everyone agrees on the answer to this question, nor on the basic approach to the epistle itself. I fall in line with those known as "revisionist thinkers" who adopt a new, non-traditional interpretation of this letter. As such, I offer a minority opinion in this section. And I thank you in advance for considering what I believe is the correct interpretation.

Historically, Protestant Reformation thinkers perceived that "Justification by Faith" was the core of Paul's letter to the Romans and used this interpretation to wrest the Church free from the clutches of erroneous Roman Catholic dogma. While sympathetic to the Protestants' needs and interests, and while ceding the importance of the Doctrine of Justification, revisionist thinkers still wonder whether writing the letter was really precipitated by Paul's need to articulate the essence of salvation. Revisionist thinkers argue it was not his primary purpose, and may not have been even a secondary one.

Paul wrote his letter to the Roman church in approximately 57AD, during his third missionary journey and apparently

# Paul's Letter to the Christians in Rome

just prior to his planned journey to Jerusalem, where he was bringing assistance to the Messianic Believers. *Issues between Jews and non-Jews are abundant in the Roman letter and betray Paul's primary reason for writing.* Jews had been banished from Rome under Claudius (Acts 18:2), but were allowed to return under Nero—the emperor who ruled when Paul wrote. This serves as an important indicator that *Paul was very much concerned with firming up relationships between Believers in Jesus who were from two separate ethnic backgrounds: Jewish Believers—who were returning from their temporary exile under Claudius—and non-Jewish Believers.*

Paul cordially greeted the church, expressed his interest in visiting soon, and gave voice to his Gospel's essence: that *Jesus is for Jews and non-Jews alike* (1:16-17). Jews and non-Jews are "in this boat together"—a "fellow*ship*" ("fellows" in the same "ship")—an idea Paul voiced when he pointed out the human sinfulness of *all* people and claimed that *Jesus can remedy the sin problem* for all. Though "saved" from sin at conversion, all *individuals*— Jewish or not—*still carry sin into the new economy* reflected by Paul in chapters 6-8. Baptism, for Paul, was a symbol of one's wanting to "walk in the newness of life," a life that brings freedom, and that was purchased by Israel's Messiah for all. Note the emphasis on *"all"* throughout Paul's argument.

Paul's explicitly dealing with matters related to Jews and Israel further underscores that Paul had Jewish and non-Jewish relationships in mind. In chapters 9-11, *Paul*

# In the Footsteps of the Rabbi from Tarsus

*tackled the question of why Jewish authorities had yet to accept Jesus,* and noted that an *acceptance was pending.* Paul revealed God's position on the Jews when he said, "My heart's desire and prayer to God for Israel" and "God has not cast away His people" the Jews (10:1 and 11:1).

After briefly addressing eschatological concerns relating to Israel, Jewish unbelief, and an eventual ingathering of non-Jewish followers of Jesus the Messiah, Paul turned his attention to *practical* considerations.

In chapter 12, he *exhorted individuals to consecrate themselves to the Lord's service,* then briefly told about the Church's ministries through which folk were to participate in advancing the Messianic Kingdom—Christ's Kingdom. He emphasized *love* and its attendant virtues and laid out a course for dealing kindly with non-believers. The Rabbi from Tarsus reflected on *relationships* with others, commenting on Believers' relationship with government authorities. He reminded saints to love their neighbors, and gave end-times instructions to be "watchful." His *practical encouragement to keep one's sinful tendencies at bay,* along with keeping in check the *tendency to judge other brothers* with differing convictions—a likely reference to those who condescended to the Jewish Believers—indicates that Paul was laboring to reconcile non-Jews and Jews in his epistle to the Romans.

# Paul's Letter to the Christians in Rome

While finalizing the personal letter, the "Apostle to the Gentiles" (Paul) shared some travel plans, noting his interest in personally visiting Jerusalem and hand carrying an offering from the Romans. In his correspondence, Paul informed the Roman Believers—comprising mostly non-Jewish members at the time of the writing—that he was "going to *Jerusalem* to minister to the saints," remarking that "it pleased those from Macedonia and Achaia" (noted previously in the Corinthian correspondence) "to *make a certain contribution for the poor among the saints who are in Jerusalem.*" As with the Corinthians, Paul intended to raise money among the Romans to assist with the apostolic work in Israel.

*The Apostle to the Gentiles loved Jews in Israel*—and made this amply clear to the Romans! Why? Arguably, Paul wanted to confront anti-Jewishness among the non-Jewish, Roman Christians. His financial appeal to the church in Rome is significant and further buttresses the point. Paul succinctly stated his position to Rome: "For if the gentiles have been partakers of their spiritual things, their *duty* is also to minister to them [the Messianic Jews in Jerusalem] in material things" (italics mine). Depending on the Bible translation you read, the term for *duty* varies: *indebted, owe, least they can do, etc.* Paul's using a term of obligation is significant, especially because it was meant to inspire non-Jewish Believers to be supportive of fledgling Messianic communities of Jewish Believers in the Land of Israel. Paul was explicit when he closed his appeal by voicing his hope that "my service for [the] *Jerusalem* [Believers] may be acceptable to the saints" there. He said, in effect: "Listen up guys. Because we have received all of our spiritual inheritance and blessings from the Jewish people, *we ought to reciprocate materially.* I am going to go to Jerusalem. I would like to carry a financial gift from you and give it to the Believers there as an expression of our support for them." I'd personally love to see more sentiment like this in the Church today.

Paul closed his letter to the Romans by offering a commendation to Phoebe, a greeting to others, a warning against false teachers, and a benediction.

## Important Interpretations

In his letter to the Romans, Paul described in detail the *all-inclusive* nature of the Gospel of Jesus Christ and explained at length that Jesus is sufficient for personal salvation. Paul gave voice to his Gospel's essence (1:16-17), noting that salvation is *for both Jews and non-Jews.* Paul noted that human sinfulness has come to all people (1:18-3:20), but that *Jesus can remedy the sin problem* for *all people*—Jews and non-Jews alike (3:21-5:21). Racism is intolerable, as are classism and sexism.

Paul, of course, was not the only disciple who was personally spreading Jesus' message and its meaning. However, he did have a unique vision that distinguished him from other Messianic advocates: Paul saw a new body consisting of *both* Jews and non-Jews, where both groups—despite their cultural differences—stood on equal footing before God, and were encouraged to stand on equal footing with each other. *This was an innovative understanding in Paul's day.*

Paul's egalitarian vision prompted him to work toward what was, at first, a strained mutual acceptance; thus *he articulated a doctrine that called for unity of confession with diversity of expression.* Would that we moderns were thus minded and less judgmental of Christians with different habits and music! Paul's innovative ideas of inclusive Christianity, for that matter, extended to women and men, and the rich and the poor. "Paul's Gospel," as he called it, did not differ from other apostles' who also emphasized Jesus' death, burial, and resurrection, and the consequential salvation made available to all—extremely important Christian basics. But his message was distinguished by the inclusive doctrine that evolved out of Paul's understanding of the Cross: that *Jesus came to give His life for a new entity, constituted by diverse people; an entity* that would eventually have global implications.

Though "saved" from sin, *individual Jews and non-Jews still carry sin into the new economy.* We see evidence of this in the anti-Semitism practiced by some of the letter's non-Jewish recipients. Paul harked to baptism as a symbol of one's leaving the "old self" behind—with its private sins and personal prejudices, re-emerging from the waters as a new and clean person, a new person in Christ (6:1-14). Paul placed a premium on living out the implications of the new life, and silencing the inclinations of the old one.

# In the Footsteps of the Rabbi from Tarsus

Of particular interest is Paul's self-disclosure: "O, wretched man that I am. Who will deliver me from this body of death?" (7:15-24). Paul recognized sin's influence—even within his apostolic self!—and personally longed for release from his sinful nature. Embracing his Lord, the Rabbi from Tarsus reminded his readers—and himself—that "there is now no condemnation to those who are in Christ Jesus" (8:1). He followed with some all-time favorite verses for Believers: "If God is for us, who can be against us?" (v. 31), "Who shall bring a charge against God's elect?" (v. 33), and "Who shall separate us from the love of Christ?" (v. 35). Who shall? Nobody. Prejudices prompt individuals to separate from one another; the Lord Himself, however, is not the least bit inclined, given the premium He places on unity.

While tossing various questions around in chapters 9-11, Paul tackled the question of why Jewish authorities had yet to accept Jesus and noted that Israel's acceptance would come in the future (11:11-32). Though many thousands of Jews had accepted Jesus as Messiah by then, *Paul was still grieved by the lack of universal and official acceptance in Judea* (9:1-5), and *troubled by the tendency of Rome's non-Jewish Christian majority to disparage the Jewish Believers* then re-entering Rome, under Nero's administration.

Paul saw God as working providentially through the Jewish disassociation from Jesus to make room for non-Jews during this season (9:30-33). But, as pleased as he was by the Gospel's expansion to *unreached* people,

# Paul's Letter to the Christians in Rome

Paul still anxiously anticipated God's fresh visitation upon Israel. *"Brethren, my heart's desire and prayer to God for Israel is that they may be saved"* (10:1).

Paul wanted individuals to place distance between themselves and their assorted base passions, to invest the better part of their energies serving the Lord—Jews and non-Jews *together*—in an orderly fashion (12:1-8).

Paul placed an emphasis on the various races learning and practicing *love* and its attendant virtues (12:9-13:10). Forsake hypocrisy, said Paul; be affectionate and kind, give honor to one another, and prefer one another. Being "diligent," "fervent in spirit," "rejoicing in hope," and "distributing [material goods] to [service] the needs of the saints" were other descriptions of desirable behavior among Believers. Paul's eschatological exhortation to be "watchful" (vv. 11-12), was followed by his practical encouragement to "walk properly" (v. 13), and to not be a "drunkard," or "lewd," and to forsake the sinful works of the flesh outright (v. 14). Being overly judgmental indicates a nature that is out of control; so Paul exhorted them by warning against the tendency to judge other brothers with differing practices and convictions (14:1-15:13)—a tacit reference to the Jewish and gentile tensions which serve as the backdrop for this letter.

## Contemporary Applications

The importance of appreciating the all-inclusive nature of the Gospel, and coming to terms with the practical outgrowths of that understanding, simply cannot be overstated. *A world wracked by social unrest and racial discrimination needs to discover the remedy made available through the Church's message of racial reconciliation.* This is the underlying sentiment of Paul's letter to the Romans—not Justification by Faith. The nuclear human family and church family are cornerstones of our particular civilization. Members of those social groups need to note the premium the Rabbi from Tarsus placed on celebrating uniformity of faith while accepting some—not all—diversity in faith, practice, and expression. While Paul advocated vociferously for fundamental truths, he also knew when to bend and appreciate diversity. Do we?

*A foundational truth for Paul—and for all Christians—is the all-inclusive nature of the Gospel and the Church,* the Church being a living expression of the Gospel. Paul articulated a vision for a Church made up of various groups—Jews and non-Jews, in the Roman case. Paul's inclusive notions extended to women and men, along with the rich and the poor. Can we make room for more people, and *other, different* people in our world? Paul thought that the Romans needed to, and we need to as well.

Even "saved" individuals *still carry sin into the new economy,* unfortunately. Paul advocated for baptism, when people publicly break with their past and leave behind the "old self" with its private sins and personal prejudices in order to emerge from the waters as a newly created person. The implication of this for the Romans

# Paul's Letter to the Christians in Rome

was the need to leave their racism in the past and become a new entity—Jews and non-Jews living and loving the Lord *together.* Does this not argue for our need to link up with others, and provide a remedy for our prejudiced world?

Paul's exhortation that individuals consecrate themselves to God, and be conformed to Him by the renewal of their minds, was important to Paul—as it indeed must be to us. His entire description of desirable Christian behavior applies today as it did yesterday: being "affectionate," "kind," giving "honor" and preference to other Believers (12:9-13:10). "Distributing [material goods] to [service] the needs of the [Jewish] saints" in Jerusalem (12:13) is an obvious practical outgrowth of inclusiveness.

All in all, instead of simply following our feelings—some of which can lead us astray with relative ease—we are encouraged to "walk properly" and not to be a "drunkard" or "lewd." Being overly judgmental is a characteristic of the flesh and so Paul warned against the tendency to judge others with differing practices and convictions (14:1-15:13).

I am particularly impressed by the premium that Paul placed on raising mission money—for the Jews in Jerusalem, in his particular case. *Would that the Church today supported the fledgling work among the Jews in Israel!* Would that the Church even supported world missions more significantly. This was on Paul's heart — not to mention God's. Where is that spirit today? *Does*

# In the Footsteps of the Rabbi from Tarsus

*the Church place a premium on assisting the Messianic movement?* Few care. Do churches invest money to support work beyond their own campuses? Not enough.

I have shared my own special interests that are stimulated through the reading of Romans. How about you? Take a moment to note your own in the following subsection.

**Personal Applications**
If you've followed the suggested pathway through this book, by this point you have read the biblical Text followed by my brief assessment of some of the more important issues in the Roman correspondence. Now let the Lord speak to your heart and use the space provided below to take stock of what the Lord is saying to you. Write down three points that seemed most meaningful to you and then in narrative form, write down how you can apply these biblical truths.

Three points that seemed most meaningful to me are:

1. _____

_____

_____

2. _____

_____

# Paul's Letter to the Christians in Rome

3. _____

_____


The lessons I learned from the three points written above
I can apply in my own life by…

_____

_____

_____

_____

_____

_____

_____

_____

_____

_____

_____

_____

_____

_____

_____

_____

## 7. Paul's Letter to Philemon

To maximize your personal spiritual growth and maturation, read *Philemon* now—before reading the sections on overview, interpretations, and contemporary applications.

### Introductory Overview

Paul's letter to Philemon was written in approximately 61 or 62AD, while Paul was imprisoned in Rome. Paul greeted the wealthy Philemon and expressed his thankfulness for their relationship. Paul *took up the case of Onesimus, a slave who had run away from Philemon's estate and who, like Philemon, eventually became a Believer in Jesus.* What ought one to do with this runaway-slave-turned-Christian-brother? What are the *ethical considerations* and *obligations*? Paul dealt with these issues in his correspondence and is seen working out practical considerations associated with his conviction that "in Christ" there was to be neither "slave nor free." This, as we know, was a core value of Paul's; so the means by which he works the concept in the real, workaday world, is instructional.

### Important Interpretations

Paul referred to Philemon as a "beloved friend," and a "fellow laborer" (v. 1). Calling him "brother" (v. 7) shows that they enjoyed a cordial relationship. A prior friendship would be needed for Paul to be bold in asking his friend to take such unprecedented action.

# Paul's Letter to Philemon

Paul appealed to Philemon on behalf of one of Philemon's runaway slaves named Onesimus (vv. 9-10). Because Philemon's former slave had become a "brother" in Christ (v. 16), the question then became: What should Philemon do? Should Philemon prosecute him under Roman law as a runaway slave? Onesimus could be crucified. Should Philemon welcome him back to the house, assuming Onesimus even wants to return? If so, on what basis? Should Philemon receive Onesimus as a non-slave, as a brother? Should Philemon take Onesimus back again as a slave, though a Christian one at that? What to do?

In his previous writings and in his speeches, Paul advocated for the Church's being a classless society where there are no Jews or Greeks, men or women, and no impoverished slaves or entitled rich, free people. *For Paul, the Church was indeed a classless society, an association of equals, a fraternity of brothers and sisters, all on equal footing, and all made free by Jesus the Messiah, God's Son.* How might these core principles of the Rabbi from Tarsus be applied in light of real-world circumstances?

It was quite a radical step, to be sure. Paul asked Philemon to cancel whatever debt Onesimus might have caused him, and to charge it to Paul's account personally (v. 18). In a somewhat gentle manner, Paul was insisting on compliance! Bold as that was, Paul's expecting Philemon to comply attests to the kind of social influence the religious leader wielded at the time; for in asking, Paul expressed expectation that his spiritual charge (Philemon) would do as Paul asked and receive his runaway slave back kindly.

## Contemporary Applications

Paul's calling a Believer a "friend" and "co-laborer" reveals a relationship that extends beyond simply "going to church together." Because relational bonds seem lacking in modernity, there is little expectation that modern church members can and will be held accountable to the Gospel's high standards. The saying that "no one will receive correction through you if they have not personally received you, first" underscores the importance of fraternal relationships as precursors to meaningful, Christian growth.

That Paul advocated for a member of society's underclass—a slave—is equally significant, and gives rise to questions about the extent to which Christians today would benefit by being engaged in social issues. Longer-established denominations have developed networks to alleviate social problems and facilitate equality. It is not at all uncommon, for example, to enter a major city and find a Catholic, Presbyterian, or Methodist hospital. The newer denominations and non-denominational ministries which have surfaced in the last century might do well to follow suit and consider how they can mobilize their influence and resources to improve humanity's existence. If not on the denomination's higher, organizational levels, at least the local church and individual Believer should investigate how Christian practice might assist Believers who find themselves in dire

# Paul's Letter to Philemon

circumstances and in need of intercessory help—like this low-class slave.

Paul's influence no doubt facilitated Philemon's resolve to do right by his former slave. Though, in a legal sense, he had every right to pursue a punitive course, his Christian virtue prompted him to take a more gracious tack. Would that we all placed a premium on lenience, on releasing debt, and on granting forgiveness when sincerely requested.

The notion of the Church as a classless society has profound implications, especially given our human tendency to stratify into higher and lower cliques based on wealth and power, beauty, prestige, education, etc. For Paul, the Christian life called for abandoning the hierarchy and replacing it with a society of equals. While there certainly are individuals more socially empowered than others, it is better that church members not be overly affected by status, causing them to discriminate on the basis of the "haves" and the "have-nots." Paul surely hated this tendency and we should disdain it too. Pauline virtue contended that it is better to let people rise and fall on their own merits, and not hold individuals back on the basis of a hierarchy.

It is worth rementioning a notion I touched on previously: *forgiveness.* Because humans tend to hold grudges, releasing someone from an infraction does not come easily. Paul knew that in releasing the guilty party, the forgiver also releases himself because he frees his energies

# In the Footsteps of the Rabbi from Tarsus

to pursue other paths and doesn't simply "stew in the juices" of discontent, no matter how legitimate his complaint might be. Forgiveness is powerful, and is an essential Christian virtue.

Those who call themselves "Christians" must accept the name's implications—that a Christian strives to be "Christ-like." Given the premium that Jesus placed on forgiveness, how can one carry His name and refuse to dispense forgiveness to a penitent person or a worthy cause? We would do well to practice the grace given us, and be more kindly disposed toward others.

### Personal Applications

If you've followed the suggested pathway through this book, by now you have read Paul's letter to Philemon followed by my brief assessment of some of the more important issues in that letter. Now let the Lord speak to your heart and use the space provided below to take stock of what the Lord is saying to you. Write down three points that seemed most meaningful to you and then in narrative form, write down how you can apply these biblical truths.

Three points that seemed most meaningful to me are:

1. _____

_____

_____

# Paul's Letter to Philemon

2. _____

_____

3. _____

_____

The lessons I learned from the three points written above I can apply in my own life by…

_____

_____

_____

_____

_____

_____

_____

_____

_____

_____

_____

_____

_____

_____

## 8. Paul's Letter to the Church at Colosse

To maximize your personal spiritual growth and maturation, read *Colossians* now—before reading the sections on overview, important interpretations, and contemporary applications.

### Introductory Overview

Paul's letter to the Colossians was dispatched along with the letter to Philemon, both of them written in approximately 61 or 62AD while the Rabbi from Tarsus was imprisoned in Rome. Following his formal introduction, *Paul extolled the preeminence of Jesus—His person and His work.* Paul articulated the Messiah's creative, redemptive work and noted how *pleased he, Paul, was to suffer* to make His work known. Rabbi Paul took on the prevailing worthless "philosophy and empty deceit" and *placed Jesus on a pedestal* high above the base notions advocated by Colossian non-believers. A declaration of the *preeminence of Jesus*—His death, burial, and resurrection—led Paul to provide a pastoral application for Believers, and close with his customary blessing.

### Important Interpretations

According to the famous writer of Colossians, the Lord has "delivered believers from the power of darkness and conveyed believers to the kingdom of His beloved Son" (1:13). This Son, said Paul, is "the image of the invisible God" (v. 15), and "the beginning, the firstborn from the dead" (v. 18). Making Him known was extremely important to Paul (vv. 24-28), who made it his aim "striving according to His working" (v. 29).

# Paul's Letter to the Church at Colosse

Apparently, there were other quasi-Christian perspectives in the marketplace of religious ideas. Paul warned: "Beware lest anyone cheat you through philosophy and empty deceit, according to the tradition of men" (2:8). He repeated the warning in v. 18, "let no one cheat you of your reward." This is a reference to the argument by some that adhering to a variety of rules would secure God's favor; rules such as "do not touch, do not taste, do not handle" (v. 21). According to Paul, following the rules has "the appearance of wisdom in self-imposed religion, false humility...but of no value against the indulgence of the flesh" (v. 23).

Jesus is sufficient to accomplish His good purposes in us and through us, said Paul, and He can do this without religious rules and impositions. Paul developed the theme of Messiah Jesus' preeminence, (3:1-4:6), asking Church folk to "put to death... fornication, uncleanness, passion, evil desire, and covetousness" (3:1-5) and to slay "anger, wrath, malice, blasphemy and filthy language," (v. 8). As "the elect of God," Believers are to replace these with tender mercies, kindness, humility, meekness, longsuffering, bearing one another's burdens, and forgiveness (vv. 12-13). Paul mentioned putting on "love" and "peace" and the benefits associated with dwelling on God's Word, to help get the better of human nature's base impulses (vv. 14-15).

The Apostle gave practical instructions—as he always did: Husbands and wives were addressed in vv. 18-19,

# In the Footsteps of the Rabbi from Tarsus

children and childrearing in vv. 20-21, and masters and slaves in 3:22-4:1.

## Contemporary Applications

The "high Christology" in Colossians is worth noting. With a high esteem of Jesus' person and work, individuals are more successful in rising up to overcome life's challenges. Why? Because if Jesus has "delivered believers from the power of darkness," and if He is "the image of the invisible God" and we have secured His attention and good favor, what are the implications for our success in life? They are boundless! Those who embrace even half of this Good News can develop a Messiah-activated confidence that will let them soar way above their highest expectations.

Believers have an inheritance and Paul warned, "Beware lest anyone cheat you through philosophy and empty deceit, according to the tradition of men." His reiterating, "let no one cheat you of your reward," tells us that something is lost when we lose our high view of Jesus, the work He accomplished, and the implications of that work for human beings who respond to it.

However, simply "believing" in Jesus intellectually is not sufficient, according to Paul. He asked that Believers *give action to conviction*—put our money/actions where our mouths are. So as not to get in the way of God's work, Believers were asked to keep their base tendencies bridled: "Put to death… fornication, uncleanness, passion, evil desire and covetousness," and subdue "wrath, malice, blasphemy, and filthy language." Better that we "put on

Christ" (Galatians 3:27), and display divinely-given characteristics like "tender mercies," genuine "kindness," sincere "humility," "meekness," "longsuffering," and the ever important resolution of "bearing one another's burdens." Foremost, Paul placed a premium on "forgiveness." *This is a recipe for success in life!*

## Personal Applications

If you've followed the suggested pathway through this book, you have now read Paul's letter to the Colossians followed by my brief assessment of some of the more important issues in that document. Now let the Lord speak to your heart and use the space provided below to take stock of what the Lord is saying to you. Write down three points that seemed most meaningful to you and then in narrative form, write down how you can apply these biblical truths.

Three points that seemed most meaningful to me are:

1. _____

_____

2. _____

_____

3. _____

_____

# In the Footsteps of the Rabbi from Tarsus

The lessons I learned from the three points written above
I can apply in my own life by…

_____

_____

_____

_____

_____

_____

_____

_____

_____

_____

_____

_____

_____

_____

_____

_____

_____

_____

_____

## 9. Paul's Letter to the Church at Ephesus

To maximize your personal spiritual maturation, read *Ephesians* in your Bible now—before reading my overview, interpretations, and contemporary applications.

### Introductory Overview

As with the previous two letters—to Philemon and the Colossians—Paul's letter to the Ephesian Believers was written approximately in 61 or 62AD, while Paul was imprisoned in Rome. Between his formal introduction and conclusion, Paul discussed *benefits* associated with following Jesus, followed by the *obligations* incumbent upon those who name the Name of the Lord.

With a premium on Christian *unity and mutual acceptance and participation,* Ephesians is referred to as a great document on the essence of the Church.

Paul said that *blessings* for Believers are to be planned by the Father, and followed with a *prayer for increased comprehension of God's grace.* How *God's grace regenerates all people who believe in Jesus*—Jews and Greeks alike—preceded a consideration of the Church being a new organism that actually *brings together Jews and non-Jews* and creates a new community through the mixture. Paul was *pleased that God gave him this unique revelation* and expressed his joy at being able to proclaim. He prayed for *increased stability,* closed the section with a doxology, and examined Believers' responsibilities in light of Jesus' work.

# In the Footsteps of the Rabbi from Tarsus

Paul's premium on *Christian unity* was developed in chapter 4, along with an *exhortation toward moral purity.* Keeping a cool-spirited and *reflective disposition* was important to Paul, especially given human nature's tendency to become inflamed. Codes of *proper conduct* were laid out in chapters 5 and 6. Mutually submissive relationships between *husbands and wives* was the object of Paul's initial concern, followed by the relationship between *parents and children,* and *masters and slaves.* After a reminder to be vigilant in *spiritual warfare,* Paul noted Tychicus' mission to bring them Paul's news.

## Important Interpretations
*Benefits* of believing and following Jesus are spelled out in the first chapter of Ephesians. Believers, said Paul, are "chosen" (v. 4), and subsequently "adopted" into God's family (v. 5)—an open family that knows not the bounds of race and culture. Being "redeemed" from sin and thus "forgiven" (v. 7) is another benefit of acceptance into this new spiritual home. Those previously alienated from God are now the objects of His pleasure and the recipients of an "inheritance" from Him as His children (v. 11) as a result of their being "sealed by the Holy Spirit" (v. 13-14). Paul was thankful for the above. He prayed that their "understanding will be enlightened" (v. 18), and that Believers might be mindful of the "hope," "riches," and "power" that constitute the inheritance promised in vv. 18-19. Paul reminded them that though previously "dead" through prior works (in a religious and moral sense), converted individuals are "alive" through Christ (2:1-9) and, as a corporate "body," are God's

# Paul's Letter to the Church at Ephesus

"workmanship" (v. 10), destined for greatness. The personal transition—from being "aliens" to being "citizens" and members of a godly commonwealth (vv. 12, 19)—comes with certain *obligations,* that Believers should be aware of, lest they fall short of God's expectations and incur His displeasure. Given all of the above, Believers are particularly expected to be "rooted and grounded in love" (3:17), an idea with many applications.

Leaving his command presence as an apostolic authority aside for the moment, in chapter 4 Paul begged Believers to "walk worthy" of their calling (v. 1), to be "lowly" and "gentle," and to demonstrate this through displays of "longsuffering" and patience with one another (v. 2). "Endeavoring to keep unity" (v. 3) is a priority now that Believers are members of one "body," have one "Spirit," and one "hope" (v. 4)—in short, we are one family. To this the Rabbi from Tarsus added that there really is only one "Lord," "faith," and "baptism" (vv. 5-6), and ultimately one "Father" making the culturally diverse Church genetically related in a spiritual sense.

Rabbi Paul accentuated One-ness, given his vision for a new organism (the Church) composed of both Jews and non-Jews (2:11-13). Previously, Paul noted, the two groups were estranged and alienated. Jesus, however, brought and bought peace (v. 14), with the result that the Church reconciles diverse peoples and personalities into one community (v. 16), now that all regenerated parties have access to God's grace (v. 18), and are called to be conduits of it themselves.

# In the Footsteps of the Rabbi from Tarsus

Paul was thrilled *that God gave him this unique revelation,* and expressed joy at being able to proclaim it to others (3:1-13). "Gentiles" becoming "fellow heirs" with Jewish Believers was a revolutionary idea in the first century; but Paul stressed that the historical tensions between the two groups were absolved and resolved in Christ.

All new creations—be they new marriages, new babies, or new businesses—are precarious and unstable at the first, and require vigilant care and attention. Paul's cosmopolitan churches were certainly no exception. Like a human father, Paul prayed for their *increased stability* (vv. 14-19), and explained Believers' responsibilities in light of Jesus' work.

Paul revisited the theme of *Christian unity* again (4:1-16), along with his ever-present *exhortations toward moral purity* (4:17-5:14). He offered encouragement— necessary in light of the prevailing lewd culture and its influence on the residents at Ephesus. In conjunction with keeping their sexual passions in check, Paul asked his new Christians to keep their anger bridled. His premium on a cool-spirited disposition is prominent in the Text from 5:22 through 6:9, where Paul advocated for moderation—emphasizing mutual acceptance and submissiveness between *husbands and wives* (vv. 22-33), between *parents and children* (6:1-4), and even between *masters and slaves* (vv. 5-9).

# Paul's Letter to the Church at Ephesus

Paul's letter ended with a reminder to the saints that he and they were all engaged in a spiritual warfare of sorts. To make his point abundantly clear, Paul borrowed the image of the Roman infantryman, describing his standard battle armaments, but giving them spiritual applications: the helmet, for example, corresponded to salvation, the sword to the Spirit and the shield to faith, to give but a few examples. After his analogy with the empire's peace-makers (soldiers), Paul expressed "peace" to the brethren, noting the "grace" given to "those who love our Lord Jesus Christ in sincerity" (vv. 23-24).

## Contemporary Applications

Much of Ephesians contains modern applications, the first being the list of *benefits* associated with "sincere" Christian faith and the actions that grow naturally from that faith. Paul employed family language—the "adoption" motif and "inheritance"—cautioning us that the personal transition from living in an isolated, self-serving state to communal membership in God's family brings certain *obligations.*

Though they neglect the *obligations,* many Christians are still pleased to claim the *promises* of the faith—an exercise in self-deceit, I feel.

Blessings from obedience follow from actual, real-world obedience, said Paul—and Moses, and virtually everyone else in the biblical record. On the other hand, those who walk contrary to the Kingdom's mandates are said to incur God's disfavor, and are not entitled to the benefits associated with membership in Christ's commonwealth. Those who walk the contrary path exclude themselves and impoverish themselves through their poor choices. Tough though this sounds, we must remember that blessings are predicated upon obedience, and do not automatically accrue because we go to church every now and then and occasionally put a few dollars in the collection plate.

Paul begged those who would listen not to ruin them-selves but to "walk worthy" and keep the resolutions they made when they first accepted Jesus. For Rabbi Paul, faithfulness meant being kind to others, being patient, and valuing unity—characteristics that, in many respects, are almost entirely lacking in North American Christianity, where people incessantly bicker and break unity without a thought to the insult and offense it bears on Christian testimony. God is not the father of this confusion!

Disoriented and selfish people emphasize the differences they have with others and stress the offenses—either real or imagined. Paul's Ephesian disciples came from different cultures and had differing dispositions and customs, and a history of insults. He envisioned the Church as a community where different and formerly hostile parties could be reconciled one to another, where peace would predominate, and where brotherly and sisterly relations would be characterized by reconciliation, rather than by dissention and dissolution.

# Paul's Letter to the Church at Ephesus

With Paul's premium on unity in mind, we should consider whether church hopping and church splitting—or any other types of human splits—offend the Gospel. When estranged parties insist that there is no means for Christians to reconcile their issues, it insults the power of Christian faith and more likely signals their own reluctance to live out the implications of the faith.

In his *exhortation toward moral purity* (4:17-5:14) we see that the Rabbi from Tarsus believed that unity comes when folk keep their base passions in check and learn to accept and forgive others—virtues in high demand but short supply in our modern culture.

Paul invoked a military image to illustrate our need to fight our negative tendencies and aggressively pursue Christian virtue. The battle equipment metaphor of a Roman infantryman is a classic teaching tool and a vivid childhood memory for many Christians.

Is the act of "going to church" by itself enough to "fight the fight" and genuinely live out the faith a person claims to embrace? No. Personal and pastoral experience has taught me that it doesn't take much for us to fall short of the New Testament's moral expectations. While we must certainly call upon God's grace to assist us with human imperfections, we should also rely upon God's standards as recorded in His Word—through Paul, in this case—to help us militantly live a Christian life. We know, of course, that our efforts will not purchase our heavenly salvation—only accepting Jesus' sacrifice can ensure that.

# In the Footsteps of the Rabbi from Tarsus

But our actions can ensure a better, more satisfying passageway through our mortal life and accrue blessings for us when we find ourselves remade and dwelling in our immortal states and estates.

## Personal Applications

If you've followed the suggested pathway through this book, by now you will have read Paul's letter to the Ephesians followed by my brief assessment of some of the more important issues in that document. Now let the Lord speak to your heart and use the space provided below to take stock of what the Lord is saying to you. Write down three points that seemed most meaningful to you and then in narrative form, write down how you can apply these biblical truths.

Three points that seemed most meaningful to me are:

1. _____

_____

2. _____

_____

_____

3. _____

_____

_____

# Paul's Letter to the Church at Ephesus

The lessons I learned from the three points written above
I can apply in my own life by…

_____

_____

_____

_____

_____

_____

_____

_____

_____

_____

_____

_____

_____

_____

_____

_____

_____

_____

## 10. Paul's Letter to the Church at Philippi

To maximize your personal spiritual growth and maturation, read *Philippians* now—before reading the sections on overview, interpretations, and contemporary applications.

### Introductory Overview

Paul's letter to the Philippians was written in approximately 62AD, while Paul was imprisoned in Rome—an experience he had, as you recall, on more than one occasion. Following his style of formal correspondence, Paul greeted the church and then shared some personal matters. *He expressed personal thankfulness* for the Philippian Believers, arguably the most *loyal* of all those he had related to in the course of his career. He voiced *confidence in the prospects for his eventual release from prison*, along with his willingness to die there—or anywhere—for Christ, should that be God's will. In a fatherly and pastoral manner, the Rabbi from Tarsus *exhorted the Philippian Believers toward worthy and fearless conduct.*

Reminding his readers—the Philippians and us—that Jesus left His palatial abode in Heaven, humbled Himself, took on human form, and *served humankind* at great personal cost, *Paul employed Jesus' example as our example for proper living*. Themes like "emptying the self" and "taking the form of a servant" epitomize Jesus' existence and remind Christian Believers—who are interested in being "Christ-like"—what it means to actually be like the self-emptying Savior. The passage in

232

# Paul's Letter to the Church at Philippi

2:1-18 gives one of the clearest descriptions of the servant Savior in the New Testament, noting that "Christ Jesus...being in the form of God, did not count equality with God a thing to be grasped, but made Himself of no reputation, taking the form of a bondservant...and being found in the appearance of a man, He humbled Himself and became obedient to the point of death, even the death of the Cross" (2:5-8). Messiah Jesus, we're told, was rewarded handsomely, receiving commendations from God His Father for a job well done. Paul told the story, in large measure, to stimulate the Philippians to take heart, reminding them that they would be handsomely rewarded at day's end for their extensions of Christian faith and virtue—as will we.

After commending Timothy and Epaphroditus and an- nouncing their upcoming visit, Paul shared how Jesus' coming had impacted his own life, causing him to *rearrange his personal priorities* in such a way that Jesus' concerns factored more significantly in Paul's constellation of personal concerns, needs, and interests. Rabbi Paul put Jesus first in his life, believing in an abiding principle that good things would come as a result—ultimately, life eternal. Paul humbly noted that he had not yet achieved his goals or his treasure, but that he continued his pursuit: "not that I have already attained it, but I press on toward the goal of Christ Jesus" (vv. 13-14). Here again, as with the example of Jesus previously, Paul gave voice to his own rearranged priorities—aligned now with his Messiah's—in order to encourage the saints.

# In the Footsteps of the Rabbi from Tarsus

Disturbed by those who interpreted the Christian Way in a manner that valued religious rituals over sound morals—contrary to the value-rich foundation he had established—Paul exhorted his audience to "join in following my example" and Jesus' by implication (3:17). Paul wanted the Philippian Believers to note and avoid the misinformed souls who walked contrary to the established Way.

Paul encouraged *unity* between Euodia and Syntyche, exhorted toward *trust,* and placed a premium on *noble thought* and *character*—always important for Rabbi Paul, who placed value in character above charisma. In closing, he expressed *thankfulness for their continual financial support* and then offered a blessing.

## Important Interpretations

That Paul was *personally imprisoned* when writing this letter is noteworthy, especially given some people's mistaken belief that Christian confessions automatically translate into immediate success and prosperity. This was obviously not the case with Paul.

His previous experiences with miseries that were "abundant," "above measure" and "frequent" were recorded in 2 Corinthians 11:23 by the Apostle, who confessed to having been "beaten" nearly to death five times (v. 24), "three times with rods," "once stoned," and even "shipwrecked" (v. 25). Paul noted "weariness and toil," "sleeplessness," "hunger and thirst" along with "cold and nakedness," further emphasizing the point: *it's not always easy being a follower*

# Paul's Letter to the Church at Philippi

*of Jesus.* Being a disciple landed Paul in prison. Those who preach the prosperity doctrine should be sued for malpractice, if not for false advertising: clearly this is not Jesus' or Paul's testimony, either by word or by personal example!

Paul was personally pressed when writing this letter. Good friends are especially appreciated during hard times—when false and shallow friends typically abandon us—and this appreciation may explain why Paul was kindly disposed toward the Philippians. Paul expected that he would be "delivered" (Philippians 1:19), but recognized that, unpleasant though his confinement was, "the things which happened to me have actually turned out for the furtherance of the Gospel" (v. 12), and for this he actually "rejoiced" (v. 18). What an optimist!

Still believing what he wrote in Romans 8:28: "all things [eventually] work for the good of those who love God"— even the seemingly bad things—Paul expressed confidence that God will "bring to completion" the "good work" He is doing within Christians (Philippians 1:6). Paul exhorted Believers to "not be terrified by [spiritually motivated] adversaries" or adversity in general (v. 28), but to maintain a deep confidence that can withstand life's storms and attacks. Being aware that God in His faithfulness will provide for us, equips Christians to better love and serve humankind. Jesus, of course, is the ultimate example, and Paul said as much in the passage we will look at next.

# In the Footsteps of the Rabbi from Tarsus

Though "in the form of God" (2:6), Jesus relinquished His regal vestments and "made Himself of no reputation, taking the form of a bondservant," (v. 7), in which capacity He came to "serve and not be served." In this, said Paul, Jesus set an example for the Philippians—and for us all. In addition, Paul was pleased to note, the "humbled" Jesus of v. 8 was finally "exalted" beyond measure in v. 9 and His glory will be manifested to all, with the result that "every knee will bow... and every tongue confess that Jesus Christ is Lord" (vv. 10-11). Good times, bad times... For Paul, it was all good because God is good; and for this reason he could say "Finally, my brethren, rejoice in the Lord" (3:1).

Paul warned about falling prey to religious legalists: "Beware of dogs, beware of evil workers," a reference to false teachers who divert attention from looking to Jesus as our ultimate hope in life (vv. 2-11).

He *encouraged unity* between two women: Euodia and Syntyche (4:1-3) and advocated for "rejoicing," saying "rejoice in the Lord always, again I say rejoice!" (v. 4). Filling up on faith—becoming "faith-full"—and adding attributes like *noble* thoughts, *just* perspectives, *virtue, and pure* and *lovely* ideas ensures that "the God of peace will be with you" (vv. 8-9).

Paul closed with a personal gloss, noting that the Philippians' "care for me has flourished" (v. 10), and that they "shared in my distress" (v. 14). He praised them: "Now you Philippians know also that in the beginning of

# Paul's Letter to the Church at Philippi

the Gospel, when I departed from Macedonia, no church shared with me concerning giving and receiving but you only" (v. 15). By way of thanks, the Apostle offered this prayer: "And my God shall supply all your need, according to His riches in Christ Jesus." (v. 19) Those of us who have experienced abandonment can take comfort in Paul's words, reminded that God doesn't abandon (even though people occasionally do) and that God does send along good friends to assist us and stand with us.

## Contemporary Applications

Paul's *imprisonment* cannot be overemphasized, because I want to impress upon my readers a firm rebuke and counterbalance to the mistaken idea that the Christian life is all about receiving boundless goodness and blessings. If one accepts that trials are blessings—albeit blessings in disguise—they may be easier to accept. Accept them we must, because it is important for us to understand that *Christian life is not always going to be easy.*

Hard times bring out the faithful friends—an extremely important lesson, especially when we distinguish true friends from false ones. If you are unsure who is "with you," consider who actually has stuck with you in tough times, and take special note of those who did even when it might have exposed them to personal risk: these are your *real* friends. Paul's friends stuck by his side when others did not; their continued financial support was an extension of their moral support. Paul noted: "You Philippians know also that in the beginning of the Gospel... no church shared

# In the Footsteps of the Rabbi from Tarsus

with me concerning giving and receiving but you only" (4:15). In v. 19, the rabbi prayed his wish out loud: "my God shall now supply all your need, according to His riches in Christ Jesus," in response to your kindness toward me.

*Will you hear Paul on this matter, and stand with your church's leadership?* In a world where people are critical of leadership, will you support your congregation's? If so, you will secure the commendation that Paul advocated in this epistle when he praised those who stood with him, while shallow Christians left his side when the going got tough.

Though Paul was abandoned by "fair weather friends," he knew that he wasn't abandoned by God. Faith prompted confidence that he would be victorious and would rise again! What work does your faith produce in you? If your disposition is increasingly optimistic, your faith is welling up; if not, you may benefit by revisiting God's promises to you. God would want you to possess a certain measure of triumphant expectation, like Paul. Without it, your energies turn inward and toward your problems—real or imagined.

Do you agree that it is better for us to invest the lion's share of our energies beyond our personal circumstances, and toward others? If so, you appreciate how personal *faith frees us up to love others* because we know that we are loved and will be taken care of, as God has promised.

# Paul's Letter to the Church at Philippi

Service in Christ's Name is important for those who claim to live for His sake—and Christians, by employing the label *"Christian,"* claim to do just that. However, many don't really live for His sake, but still claim the benefits that accrue to those who do. Can one derive benefit by actually taking on a servant role every now and again? Of course. Churches should help Christians take on these servant roles by teaching the importance of Christian service, and by helping implement that service. Failure to do so enables Christians to live in their spoiled states—an American problem, to be sure. Christian growth is stunted when individuals remain as self-centered and spoiled infants in the faith, if they have any real faith at all.

Serving and working beyond ourselves does not excuse us from allowing the Lord to work within us. Keeping a good attitude is important, given that people—even good people—possess the ability to "fuss," as did Euodia and Syntyche, whom Paul encouraged to get along. Because incessant fretting can bring down our inner constitutions, Paul advocated that we "rejoice in the Lord always." Do we do this? And do we keep ahold of other characteristics, like nobility? Do we place a premium on justice? Do we keep our hearts and minds with pure thoughts? Or do we trample virtue through self-indulgent vice? If so, we are in trouble. If not, we can experience the "God of peace" whom Paul said "will be with" us as a result.

# In the Footsteps of the Rabbi from Tarsus

## Personal Applications

If you've followed the suggested pathway through this book, by now you will have read Paul's letter to the Philippians followed by my brief assessment of some of the more important issues in that document. Now let the Lord speak to your heart and use the space provided below to take stock of what the Lord is saying to you. Write down three points that seemed most meaningful to you and then in narrative form, write down how you can apply these biblical truths.

Three points that seemed most meaningful to me are:

1. _____

   _____

   _____

2. _____

   _____

   _____

3. _____

   _____

   _____

# Paul's Letter to the Church at Philippi

The lessons I learned from the three points written above
I can apply in my own life by...

_____

_____

_____

_____

_____

_____

_____

_____

_____

_____

_____

_____

_____

_____

_____

_____

## 11. Paul's 1ˢᵗ Letter to Timothy

To maximize your spiritual growth and maturation, read *1 Timothy* in your Bible now—before reading my overview, important interpretations, and contemporary applications.

### Introductory Overview

Paul's first canonical letter to Timothy was written from Macedonia in approximately 63 or 64AD, following Paul's imprisonment. After his introduction, Paul *warned against destructive false teachings* and offered his vision for a healthy, growing Church. As the first order of business, Paul instructed how *prayer* should be conducted, gave an *exhortation to modesty* and self-control, and spelled out *essential characteristics for high quality leaders:* bishops, elders, and deacons. Having addressed these initial concerns, Paul discussed the need for Timothy to *keep to the orthodox faith* delivered to him, and not to be swayed by novel doctrines that aren't rooted in standard apostolic teaching. Paul talked about *pastoring different people at different stages of life:* men and women, the young and the old, widows, elders, and slaves. These understandings were deemed authoritative. Paul exhorted Timothy to *lead by example* and warned the wealthy not to be too haughty.

### Important Interpretations

Paul's *warning against destructive false teachings* (1:3-11) is noteworthy, especially given the tendency in our novelty-saturated culture to follow entertaining fads. Novel and entertaining doctrines might seem innocent enough, as they provide seemingly harmless entertainment

# Paul's 1ˢᵗ Letter to Timothy

for bored masses of Christian consumers; but, teachings that run contrary to the apostolic tradition must be eschewed, given that "a little leaven leavens the whole lump" (1 Corinthians 5:6; Galatians 5:9)

Paul underscored this point by emphatically urging Timothy to "charge some that they *teach no other doctrine*" (1 Timothy 1:3). At issue for Paul were erroneous teachings that placed a premium on "fables" that "cause disputes" and that stood in the way of "godly edification" (v. 4). The mandate to hold these at bay is as true and necessary now as when Paul first put pen to paper many years ago. Paul explicitly told Timothy that the Christian's primary purpose, and the actual by-product of good doctrine, is stimulating "love from a pure heart, from a good conscience, and sincere faith" (v. 5). Disputes over petty teachings were distractions at best, and hazards at the worst. Whatever the actual case, Paul felt that they contributed nothing toward the faith's essence (vv. 3-11) and ought to be avoided.

After noting what needed to be shunned, Paul voiced what needed to be embraced. Paul advocated for *prayer* in 2:1-7; for all men generally (v. 1), and for all those in "authority" particularly (v. 2). Instructions for calm and good order (v. 8-15) included a premium on men having a generally peaceful disposition (v. 8) and women exercising self-control through "modesty," "propriety," and "moderation" (v. 9), which Paul said is "proper for women professing religion" (v. 10). Paul saw merit in a disciplined life.

# In the Footsteps of the Rabbi from Tarsus

While speaking about matters of personal self-control, the Rabbi from Tarsus preferred that wives work alongside their husbands and assume leadership roles in that capacity—leadership being the nature of males (vv. 11-14). This, said Paul, is preferred over women taking the lead in affairs, a position that typically does not bide well with males, given that it runs contrary to their natural inclinations and dispositions.

Paul's saying "women will be saved in childbearing, if they continue in faith, love, and holiness, with self-control" (v. 15) is grounds for hearty discussion. What did Paul mean? Was he saying that women have a diminished value in God's economy, and that they find their primary purpose in the bedroom and the home—merely as servants to the dominant males? Some say "yes"; others "no." I do *not* advocate for a diminished view of womanhood.

Because Paul, more than anyone else in biblical literature, advocated for women's rights and privileges—as equal citizens alongside men, and as fellow ministers of the Gospel—some are understandably shocked to discover the statements in 11-15. Given the usual tone of equality in Pauline thought noted elsewhere, there seems no reason to assume that he suddenly changed here to a course where he thenceforth relegated women's purposes to the fruits of the bedroom—and nothing else. How are we to read Paul, in this case?

Before jumping to conclusions, we need to consider what Paul might have meant by saying "saved," as in "saved through childbearing," and then consider the possible applications for the women of his time, and the implications for us.

This statement that women will find "salvation" in the bearing and rearing of children is controversial to the core. But, "save" can mean to be "made whole," and needn't refer only to having one's "soul saved"—this is the first (mis)understanding. Might Paul have had *wholeness* in mind?

In Genesis, we're told that a lonely and incomplete Adam found his helper in Eve, with whom he became "one flesh" (Genesis 2:18-24, esp. v. 24). Their inter-relatedness was the object of Moses' attention in the Genesis Text. Here, in 1 Timothy, while harking back to Adam and Eve in The Garden, Paul took up the matter of the inter-relatedness between life partners, a matching process that, in biblical days, was initiated by the males of the species. Inasmuch as a wife's biological fruitfulness comes naturally through working together with her husband— and legitimate growth is impossible without his active participation—so too spiritual fruitfulness results naturally through association and participation with the men. In Paul's day, his concern with women in the church centered on some pushy "spiritual" women, who marginalized the men and brought forth their spiritual baggage. Much of what he wrote was directed to help Timothy deal with these prophetesses. As it takes both a man and a woman to bring a God-created child into the world, Paul taught that strong-willed wives need to work alongside their husbands, mindful that the excessively independent and strong-willed woman can really only accomplish her God-ordained spiritual fruitfulness and purpose with the man in her life, and not distinct from him.

Perhaps concern over Roman religious practices led Greek historian Plutarch (46-120AD) to advise newlyweds that "it is becoming for a wife to worship and to know only the gods that her husband believes in, and to shut the front door tight upon all queer rituals and outlandish superstitions. For with no god do stealthy and secret rites performed by a woman find any favor" *(Advice To The Bride And Groom)*. In any event, in like manner Paul advocated for agreement between marriage partners and noted that problems arise when it is missing.

Having addressed the conduct of men and women in worship, Paul spelled out some essential characteristics for bishops/elders (3:1-7), and then deacons (vv. 8-13).

It was not unreasonable for Rabbi Paul to expect (require!) that congregational leaders, being public examples by virtue of their public positions, be exemplary in their personal lives and not just in their professional ones. Nobody is perfect, to be sure; so, in requiring that they be "blameless" (3:2), he did not demand perfection. What then? At issue was keeping their reputations unsullied by a history of unbridled appetites.

A leader's being known as the "husband of one wife" (v. 2), paints the picture of a man who has himself and his business under control. Paul underscored this by adding that he also must be "temperate, sober minded, of good behavior, hospitable...not given to wine, not violent, not greedy for money, but gentle, not quarrelsome, not covetous" (v. 3). Deacons, in like manner, must display reasonable control: "reverent, not double-tongued, not given to much wine, not greedy for money" (v. 8). Paul considered proper personal and social decorum important: He placed a premium on it both here and elsewhere (cf. 5:1-6:21). In all cases, *self-control is required*—for both men and women. Before one can lead the Church, one must be able to lead one's own self by having personal and family business attended to properly!

Paul next discussed the need for Timothy, a leader himself, to *keep to the orthodox faith* delivered to him, and not to give way to novel-sounding doctrines and approaches to spirituality that were not previously sanctioned by the apostolic seal. Paul was aware of religious innovations proffered by unauthorized individuals who were out of control and dangerous (3:14-4:16)—"wolves in sheep's clothing," to borrow one of Jesus' expressions (Matthew 7:15).

Paul said that these had "depart[ed] from the faith" (1 Timothy 4:1), and that—though they might at face value, sound impressive—they really speak "lies and hypocrisy" (v. 2). Their legalistic speech is really driven by "deceitful spirits" and by "demons" (vv. 1, 3). The Rabbi from Tarsus said that these teachings should be confuted and "rejected" by Timothy (v. 7), who was to "command and teach" worthy and sound doctrine (v. 11) and to lead the

Believers by his own example "in word, in conduct, in love, in spirit, in faith, in purity" (v. 12).

Could noble Timothy skid off the road of righteousness and become a traffic fatality on the religious and moral highway of life? Yes, he most certainly could. Paul said as much: "*Take heed to yourself* [Timothy,] and to the doctrine. Continue in them, for in doing this you will save both yourself and those who hear you" (v. 16). To stress his warning, Paul closed the personal letter with a more emotional and emphatic appeal: "O Timothy! Guard what was committed to your trust, avoiding the profane and idle babblings and contradictions of what is falsely called knowledge—by professing it some have strayed concerning the faith. Grace be with you. Amen" (6:20-21). If Timothy, noble as he was, could fall victim to the ravages of human sinfulness, what about the rest of us? We can too. God help us!

## Contemporary Applications
How can we guard our hearts and minds today? How can we not be overly impressed by counterfeit religious voices and persuasions, or overrun by human sinfulness, generally? Personal knowledge of the Scriptures is a great start. Educational standards for religious leaders, likewise, would provide some insurance that their messages display fidelity to the historic and apostolic Christian faith. Even minimal standards guard against them unleashing their imaginations on biblical Texts, and giving voice to the results in the name of "the leading of the Spirit." Our novelty-seeking culture has a tendency to follow charismatic

individuals peddling entertaining fads; a special vigilance is called for.

Novel and entertaining doctrines surface from interesting visionaries who advocate for one or another supposedly revealed truth. Nonsense is packaged and promoted by savvy entrepreneurs, and religious consumers "buy into" their religious concoctions to the tune of hundreds of millions of dollars. Paul would not be pleased. His emphatically "urging" that Timothy "charge some that they teach no other doctrine," stresses the importance of staying within the purview of genuine, canonical, apostolic teaching.

Paul spoke of Christian-sounding "fables." Have you run across these, or possibly bought into any in the course of your Christian life? Bad doctrine ultimately feeds bad appetites and leads to bad conduct. Good teaching, as Paul stated at the outset of this letter, stimulates "love from a pure heart, from a good conscience and sincere faith," and leads toward righteousness and spiritual productivity. This, of course, is to be preferred.

Paul advocated for *prayer*—for all men generally, and for all those in "authority" particularly—and placed a premium on calm and good order. Prayer, itself, is typically the work product of someone who believes that God exists and is concerned for His people; it also reflects that a petitioner has decided to put his or her hope in God instead of their own abilities. Personal prayer requests usually evolve out of some combination of the above.

# In the Footsteps of the Rabbi from Tarsus

Though ordinary people do well to petition God for their challenges, in his letter to Timothy, Paul dealt with prayer for those who lead—civil leaders particularly.

When we consider the behavior of godless Roman civic and military leaders in Paul's time, we have to conclude that we are supposed to respect legitimate authorities, whether or not we appreciate all of their policies. Requiring prayer for civil authorities tacitly suggests that Christians are to be good citizens, dutifully submitting to the state's legitimate mandates and agents. If this is the case, why do Christians—in the name of virtue—disobey laws, bash presidents and governors, and the like? Disrespect is as rampant in the Church as in the culture! This should not be. Christians "take shots" not only at civic leaders, but also at their own—Church leaders! Paul would not be at all pleased by this, as it flies in the face of the Christian virtue he taught.

We all must live under some manner of lordship. There are no exceptions, no exemptions. God, of course, is the ultimate Lord and Overseer, though on Earth, communities have designated worldly leaders—all of whom will eventually give an account to an omnipotent God. Families—microcosms of the larger regnant culture—also must have structure and accountability. Though families are patriarchal in nature, mutual and fair submission between husbands and wives is the precondition for an orderly household, where cooperation brings success more than does dominance or competition. Dominant and submissive themes—between men and women and masters and slaves—really are immoral and don't lead to success, especially in the modern era.

With so much abuse, abandonment, and relational wreckage in our culture—often attributable to the abysmal performance of males—it is little wonder that women increasingly envision success in life as independent of men. For some, and for understandable reasons, dependency seems like a recipe for disaster. Though we must be sympathetic, we must still consider the Texts where Paul advised that women will find their *ultimate* fulfillment in life through their relationships with males, just as men will do so with women, for the same reasons.

Independence will not work. *Inter*dependence will!

In Bible times, success in life, to a certain extent, came by means of well-intended life partners who engaged in a mutually dependent relationship. In biblical times and with biblical virtue, that relationship was initiated by the proactive males of the species—who took the lead—with the females serving as the "chosen ones." Much as the chosen wife's biological fruitfulness (children) was understood as a natural by-product of her relationship with her husband, so too was spiritual fruitfulness construed by Paul as the natural result of working with men and not something achieved apart from them. Generally speaking—though there may be some exceptions—in the local church, a woman married to a strong Christian man will always stand a better chance of extending her sphere of spiritual and relational influence than will a single woman not connected to a male leader, no matter how talented she may be.

After delineating the preferred relationship for success, Paul described bishops and deacons—the men who, with the women above, were to exemplify the faith and conduct Paul wanted espoused and modeled.

Though polygamy was sanctioned in the ancient biblical world, and though sexual relationships outside marriage were accepted in the Greco-Roman culture, Paul would have none of either for Believers. As heads of a counter-cultural movement, the Church's leaders needed to display characteristics that outperformed the prevailing culture. Temperance, sober-mindedness, and hospitality are but some of the characteristics that are noteworthy in the Text, as are calm dispositions and controlled appetites. Having the tongue in check was desirable, as was reverence. Over all, self-control was of prime importance. All are desirable characteristics even today.

Because sound conduct and sound doctrine go hand in hand, Paul went on to discuss the need for Timothy, a Church leader, to *keep to the orthodox faith* passed on to him, and not to adopt novel-sounding doctrines that were not approved by the apostolic leadership. There were and still are many entertaining options; we need to remember that "departing from [true] faith" has hazardous consequences.

# Paul's 1st Letter to Timothy

## Personal Applications

If you've followed the suggested pathway through this book, by now you will have read Paul's first letter to Timothy followed by my brief assessment of some of the more important issues in that document. Now let the Lord speak to your heart and use the space provided below to take stock of what the Lord is saying to you. Write down three points that seemed most meaningful to you and then in narrative form, write down how you can apply these biblical truths.

Three points that seemed most meaningful to me are:

1. _____

_____

_____

2. _____

_____

_____

3. _____

_____

_____

# In the Footsteps of the Rabbi from Tarsus

The lessons I learned from the three points written above
I can apply in my own life by...

_____

_____

_____

_____

_____

_____

_____

_____

_____

_____

_____

_____

_____

_____

_____

_____

_____

_____

_____

## 12. Paul's Letter to Titus

To maximize your spiritual growth and maturation, read *Titus* in your Bible now—before reading my overview, interpretations, and contemporary applications.

### Introductory Overview

Paul wrote his personal letter to Titus between 63 and 64AD, while Paul was en route to Nicopolis after being released from his first imprisonment in Rome. After his formal introduction, as in his first letter to Timothy, *Paul commended the appointment of leaders*, and *listed attendant qualifications.* He expressed his *interest in holding false teachers at bay* and gave his standard *exhortation toward good conduct.*

### Important Interpretations

Paul's requirements for leaders (1:5-9) were—and remain— much the same as those noted previously in 1 Timothy. Paul's wanting the church "set in order" (v. 5), is followed by the qualifications of a stable family, not being too "self-willed" or "quick-tempered," "violent," "greedy," and the like. The issue is that leaders who can attend to their own personal affairs are better able to attend to the church's business—the growth and well-being of the membership.

Bothered by the "many insubordinate," "idle talkers" and "deceivers" (v. 10), the Rabbi from Tarsus stated that they needed silencing (v. 11); for, though they professed to know God they were, in truth, "abominable," "disobedient" and "disqualified for every good work" (v. 16). By way of

contrast, Titus "had the goods," as they say. In addition
to personally appointing solid leaders (1:5-9), he was to
"teach sound doctrine" (2:1) and to exhort the church's
membership toward good conduct (vv. 2-10).

> For the grace of God that brings salvation has
> appeared to all men teaching us that, denying
> ungodliness and worldly lusts, we should live
> soberly, and righteously, and godly in the present
> age, looking for the blessed hope and glorious
> appearing of our great God and Savior Jesus Christ,
> who gave Himself for us, that He might redeem us
> from every lawless deed and purify for Himself His
> own special people, zealous for good works.—
> 2:11-14

An exhortation worth remembering!

Paul continued to instruct Titus what to convey to the
Believers: "be subject to rulers and authorities" (3:1) and
not act like unregenerate heathen, being "foolish,
disobedient, deceived, serving various lusts and pleasures,
living in malice and envy, hateful and hating one another"
(v. 3).

## Contemporary Applications
Paul presented the same list of quality characteristics in
Titus as he did in 1 Timothy, an indication that he was
advocating core values of his. For Paul, public victories
(as with the leadership of elders and deacons) came in

the wake of private victories. One must win the battle over the self before one is qualified to assist others in advancing in their lives and faith! This point is abundantly clear and important, even for those not called to be Christian leaders.

Much as Titus was to "set in order" the churches, so too might some of us need to get aspects of our own lives on better footing, "in order"—that is, in God's order. Given that *the most formidable foe we will ever contend with is our self,* we do well to get a hand on our human tendency to be "self-willed," "quick-tempered," "violent," "greedy," and the like. These impulses are like fire that, if not controlled, can escalate and burn down entire forests.

Christians are to engage in a struggle, and the war does have a casualty list—one that is way too long. If we fail to attend to the darker side of our nature, privately, we may wind up being embarrassed when our foibles become public. Add to this the promised exposure on "Judgment Day," and the momentary pleasure of sin loses its appeal.

Paul saw the real spiritual battle as between "flesh" and "Spirit," and not between one religious tradition and another. Whether someone keeps particular dietary laws or observes a particular holiday will not contribute toward their victory over the adversary of self. However, possessing an inner resolve to fight against our sinful nature will let virtue emerge triumphant.

# In the Footsteps of the Rabbi from Tarsus

For the Rabbi from Tarsus, church services held on a Saturday or a Sunday really was not the issue. But not everyone agreed with Paul.

Some argued that keeping particular rules translated into better spirituality—"legalists," whom Paul called "insubordinate," "idle talkers," and "deceivers;" people he did not take seriously himself. He *was* concerned that others might accept their mistaken notions. In order for them and us to know his thoughts on the matter, Paul was vociferous, noting that these teachers are "abominable," "disobedient," and "disqualified for every good work."

Though many today criticize Paul for being too harsh and dogmatic, we should appreciate his "straight talking." Too many ministers are afraid to be direct—afraid of offending. So what! People may need to be stirred and offended.

In one of the most uplifting passages in the New Testament, Paul revealed that "The grace of God has appeared to all men" (2:11). There is a mercy and grace that extends to all people—women and men alike—irrespective of past sins. When in the throes of despair, we need to know that there is a "grace," a mercy available, should we opt to reach for it. In any event, God is reaching down with His grace: it costs nothing to receive it, but it costs something to keep it and extend it outward. In 2:12, Paul said that God is "teaching us that, denying ungodliness and worldly lusts, we should live soberly and righteously and godly in the present age...."

# Paul's Letter to Titus

Here, the premium is placed on "denying ungodliness and worldly lusts" in view of the grace given. Now that we know what is made available, we are instructed to refocus our energies by "looking for the blessed hope and glorious appearing of our great God and Savior Jesus Christ." When we invest our energies in advancing Christ's Kingdom we experience a transformation that is unique to the Christian experience.

Jesus "gave Himself for us, that He might redeem us from every lawless deed and purify for Himself His own special people, zealous for good works." Apparently *the Lord wants to get some mileage out of His people.* He wants to redeem us from a sinful and decadent state, and use us as a testimony to His grace and goodness.

Because evidence of the transformed life is gleaned from the way Believers interact with others, Paul exhorted that folk "be subject to rulers and authorities." If Paul regarded good citizenship as extremely important, we may do well to examine our own performance in this area. Of course, it is easier to be a good citizen if one supports the president or political party that holds power. What are our obligations when we disagree with a particular administration or policy? Happily, in our culture there are venues to express discontent, and Christians should exercise their prerogatives. Still, maintaining a respectful posture toward legitimate authority is necessary to maintain an untarnished Christian testimony.

# In the Footsteps of the Rabbi from Tarsus

## Personal Applications

If you've followed the suggested pathway through this book, by now you will have read Paul's letter to Titus followed by my brief assessment of some of the more important issues in that document. Now let the Lord speak to your heart and use the space provided below to take stock of what the Lord is saying to you. Write down three points that seemed most meaningful to you and then in narrative form, write down how you can apply these biblical truths.

Three points that seemed most meaningful to me are:

1. _____

_____

_____

2. _____

_____

_____

3. _____

_____

_____

# Paul's Letter to Titus

The lessons I learned from the three points written above
I can apply in my own life by...

_____

_____

_____

_____

_____

_____

_____

_____

_____

_____

_____

_____

_____

_____

_____

_____

_____

_____

_____

## 13. Paul's 2nd Letter to Timothy

Finally, the last letter! To maximize your personal spiritual growth and maturation, read *2 Timothy* in you Bible now—before reading my overview, important interpretations, and contemporary applications.

### Introductory Overview

Paul's second letter to Timothy was written between 66 and 67AD, *just before Paul's death.* In it, Paul greeted Timothy and *encouraged Timothy to be strong.* Timothy's natural tendency to fear may have been exacerbated by Paul's dire circumstances at the time. Paul exhorted his chosen leader to be *bold* in the face of opposition and appealed for Timothy to visit. Paul *shared news of God's assistance in his distress* and then shared his final greetings. This is our last word from Paul and brings to a close our considerations of the travels and teachings of the Rabbi from Tarsus.

### Important Interpretations

Paul needed to encourage Timothy to be strong, confirming our suspicions that leaders are not perfect and sometimes even they need help to overcome weaknesses.

Arguably, Timothy had a predisposition toward fear, which, if left unchecked, could have been his personal undoing (1:3-2:7). Paul's exhortation to the young leader to be *bold* in the face of opposition (2:8-4:8) reminds us that we must push ourselves at times—and sometimes even push others gently—given our tendency to shrink back from advancing in our Christian lives. Paul noted that there is heavenly assistance (4:14-18), another reminder that we don't walk through our trials alone; we can call on help from the One who said "I am with you to the end of the age." (Matthew 28:20)

Shortly after sharing this note, Paul, who once belonged to the Church, faded away only to belong to history. But he lives in the memory of those who care to consider his way by considering his words.

## Contemporary Applications
The exhortation in 2:1-4:8 to be bold in the face of opposition has broad applications that are germane to the Christian experience, given that we do not go through life unopposed. Again, Paul pointed out that those who possess Christian virtue need to marshal the resources necessary to perform boldly, in spite of our tendencies to shrink away. Paul exhorted us to be bold for the Gospel.

## Personal Applications
If you've followed the suggested pathway through this book, by now you will have read Paul's second letter to Timothy followed by my brief assessment of some of the more important issues in that document. Now let the Lord speak to your heart and use the space provided below to take stock of what the Lord is saying to you. Write down three points that seemed most meaningful to you and then in narrative form, write down how you can apply these biblical truths.

# In the Footsteps of the Rabbi from Tarsus

Three points that seemed most meaningful to me are:

1. _____

   _____

   _____

2. _____

   _____

   _____

3. _____

   _____

   _____

The lessons I learned from the three points written above I can apply in my own life by...

_____

_____

_____

_____

_____

_____

_____

# Paul's 2<sup>nd</sup> Letter to Timothy

# Conclusion

## Final Reflections on Pauline Faith and Practice

At the outset, I held out promise that this book would provide a service to individuals interested in being refreshed and transformed. Assuming that you followed the assignments and did the homework throughout—by filling in the spaces where you were asked to note special insights that *you* gleaned from *your* encounter with Pauline literature—I trust that you now are in a position to gather up your raindrops in your own drinking glass. Here is what I now propose: Go back and review the assignment sections in the previous chapters. Make special notes of what you considered to be *most significant* to *you personally*, and note those in the following pages. Take the time to (1) reflect upon your

# In the Footsteps of the Rabbi from Tarsus

responses to Paul's exhortations, (2) note your impressions of those teachings and your responses, below, and (3) follow with a personal commitment to yourself and to your Lord.

Here I basically want you to write your own conclusion to the book. I hope that for you the end will be a new beginning. In any case, instead of telling you what to think, I want to thank you for going on the journey with me to and through Paul's words and world, and for reflecting upon what I think. Having done so, I really think that you are now in a position to speak for yourself. Do it!

Go ahead and wrap this up for yourself now. The blessings will come, according to Christ's promises.

_____

_____

_____

_____

_____

_____

_____

_____

# Conclusion

_____

_____

_____

_____

_____

_____

_____

_____

_____

_____

_____

_____

_____

_____

_____

_____

_____

_____

_____

_____

# In the Footsteps of the Rabbi from Tarsus

_____

_____

_____

_____

_____

_____

_____

_____

_____

_____

_____

_____

_____

_____

_____

_____

_____

_____

_____

_____

# Conclusion

_____

_____

_____

_____

_____

_____

_____

_____

_____

_____

_____

_____

_____

_____

_____

_____

_____

_____

_____

_____

# In the Footsteps of the Rabbi from Tarsus

# Conclusion

_____

_____

_____

_____

_____

_____

_____

_____

_____

_____

_____

_____

_____

_____

_____

_____

_____

_____

_____

_____

_____

# In the Footsteps of the Rabbi from Tarsus

_____

_____

_____

_____

_____

_____

_____

_____

_____

_____

_____

_____

_____

_____

_____

_____

_____

_____

_____

_____

_____

_____

# Conclusion

_____

_____

_____

_____

_____

_____

_____

_____

_____

_____

_____

_____

_____

_____

_____

_____

_____

_____

_____

_____

_____

# In the Footsteps of the Rabbi from Tarsus

_____

_____

_____

_____

_____

_____

_____

_____

_____

_____

_____

_____

_____

_____

_____

_____

_____

_____

_____

_____

_____

_____

_____

_____

# Conclusion

_____

_____

_____

_____

_____

_____

_____

_____

_____

_____

_____

_____

_____

_____

_____

_____

_____

_____

_____

_____

_____

# In the Footsteps of the Rabbi from Tarsus

278

# Conclusion

_____

_____

_____

_____

_____

_____

_____

_____

_____

_____

_____

_____

_____

_____

_____

_____

_____

_____

_____

_____

_____

_____

# In the Footsteps of the Rabbi from Tarsus

_____

_____

_____

_____

_____

_____

_____

_____

_____

_____

_____

_____

_____

_____

_____

_____

_____

_____

_____

_____

_____

_____

_____

_____